THE COMPLETE LIBRARY SKILLS
Grade 6

By
Linda Turrell

Cover and Inside Illustrations by
Darcy Myers

Publishers
T.S. Denison & Company, Inc.
Minneapolis, Minnesota 55431

Standard Book Number: 513-02213-9
The Complete Library Skills—Grade 6
Copyright © 1994 by T.S. Denison & Co., Inc.
9601 Newton Avenue South
Minneapolis, Minnesota 55431

Printed in the USA

TABLE OF CONTENTS

Welcoming Sixth Graders to the Library 4
The Dewey Decimal System 5
The Dewey Decimal System-Using It Well 6
The Dewey System-The 100 Divisions 7
Dewey Decimal Activity 8
Understanding the "Decimal" in the
   Dewey Decimal System 9-10
Putting Call Numbers in Order 11
Research Situations 12
Dewey Decimal-Research Situations 13
Research Situation Activity 14
What Division Do You Need? 15
What Dewey Subject Division? 16

Using The Card Catalog-Choosing a Card 17
Comparing Cards - Activities 18-19
Comparing Catalog Cards - Overview 20
Card Catalog - Research Situations 21
What Catalog Card Do You Need? Activities 22-24
Name That Card 25
Choose Your Card 26

Comparing Encyclopedia Indexes 27
Comparing Encyclopedia Indexes–Transportation 28
Comparing Encyclopedia Indexes–Hobbies 29

Using a Magazine Guide 30

Introduction to Research 31
Brainstorming 32
Choosing Your Topic 33
Choosing Topics - Activities 34-35
Getting Ready for Research 36
Dictionary Bank 37
Choosing Sources 38-39

The Reader's Guide to Periodical Literature 40
Using a Magazine Guide Activities 41-43

Using a Book Index 44
Book Index Activities 45-47

Almanac 48
Using the Almanac 49
Using the Almanac Activity 50
Using the Almanac - Overview 51

Atlas 52
Biographical Dictionary 52
Vertical File 52
Using the Biographical Dictionary 53

Preliminary Research 54
Cautionary Notes on Preliminary Research 55
Preliminary Research Checklist 56

Charts, Time Lines, and Tables 57
Finding Information from Charts 57
Activities Using Summary Charts 58-59

Finding Information from Time Lines 60
Activities Using Time Lines 61-63
My Own Time Line 64
Fining Information from Tables 65
Activities Using Tables 66-67

Skimming 68
Skimming Activity 69
Freewriting 70
Freewriting Questions 71

Taking Notes 72
3"x5" Reproducible Note Taking Cards 73
4"x6" Reproducible Note Taking Cards 74
Reproducible Bibliography Note Taking Cards 75
Note Taking Tips 76

Organizing an Outline 77
Outline Tips 78
Outline Diagram 79

Evaluating Your Research: Fact or Opinion? 80
Is it Fact or Opinion Activities 81-82

Supporting Your Research Statements 83
Supporting Your Research Statements-Activities 84-85
Supporting Your Research Statements-Overview 86

Writing Your Report 87
Checklist for Writing Your Report 88

Writing the Footnote - The Book 89
Writing the Footnote - The Book Activities 90-91
Writing the Footnote - The Magazine 92
Writing the Footnote - The Magazine Activities 93-94
Writing the Footnote - The Encyclopedia 95
Writing the Footnote - The Encyclopedia Activities .. 96-97

Writing the Bibliography - The Book 98
Writing the Bibliography - The Book Activities 99-100
Writing the Bibliography - The Magazine 101
Writing the Bibliography -
   The Magazine Activities 102-103
Writing the Bibliography - The Encyclopedia 104
Writing the Bibliography -
   The Encyclopedia Activities 105-106
Bibliography Review Chart 107

Proofing Your Report 108

The Mystery 109
List of Mysteries 110
Mystery Activities 111-112
Classic Children's Literature 113
List of Classics 114
Classic Children's Literature Activities 115-117
Reading Incentives for Grade Six 118
Suggested Authors for Sixth Grade 119
The Glossary 120-123

WELCOMING SIXTH-GRADERS TO THE LIBRARY

The sixth grade student has already learned a great deal about the library and the wealth of materials that can be found there. *The Complete Library Skills — Grade Six,* provides a good review in the first part of the book which covers the Dewey Decimal System, the card catalog, magazines, encyclopedias, indexes, and other review topics.

The primary focus of *The Complete Library Skills — Grade Six,* is "research." Sixth grade is a time when elementary students are maturing and preparing for the transition to Junior High. This is a wonderful time to help these students learn how to use the library and its reference materials for writing research reports. In *The Complete Library Skills — Grade Six,* the children will learn how to choose a topic; brainstorm topic ideas; prepare for researching the topic; use reference materials (almanac, biographical dictionary, encyclopedias, atlas, vertical files); how to use time lines, summary charts and tables; how to take notes; organize an outline; evaluate research and support research statements; and how to write a footnote and bibliography.

In the final section of *The Complete Library Skills — Grade Six,* the children will be encouraged to read mystery stories and will learn what makes a good mystery. Following the mysteries, the children will be introduced to the world of "children's classic literature." Sixth grade is an excellent time to motivate children to read some of the world's greatest pieces of literature, such as *Huckleberry Finn* and *Black Beauty.*

THE DEWEY DECIMAL SYSTEM –

Sometimes you will visit your library and ask: Where do I begin to look? What section of the Dewey System do I need to check? How do you decide what section of the Dewey System will help you? You must always analyze your research situation. Ask yourself three questions:

What do I really need?

Where can I find it?

How much information do I want?

Let's look at an example. You are looking for information about space travel and satellites. What do you need? You need information about space satellites. Where can you find it? Look at the Dewey chart. The 600-699 section (Useful Arts) has books about transportation including space. Now how much information do you need? You need enough information for a report. So at least two or three books will help.

It is also a good idea to clearly define your research topic. If you are clear about the subject, it will be easier to choose a Dewey section. Let's look at some research situations on page 12. See if you can choose a Dewey division to help you.

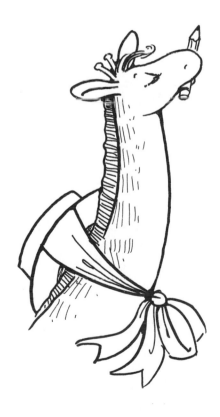

THE DEWEY DECIMAL SYSTEM – USING IT WELL

You are aware of the Dewey Decimal System, but let's review it. The Dewey Decimal System is one system that arranges books in ten divisions. A book is given a call number which includes the Dewey number and the first two letters of the author's last name. The books are then arranged in number order first and alphabetical order second.

Here is a Dewey Decimal System chart to help you review the ten sections of the library.

000 - 099	**GENERAL REFERENCE** – (Atlas, Dictionary, Encyclopedia)
100 - 199	**PHILOSOPHY & PSYCHOLOGY**– (Ideas of Humankind)
200 - 299	**RELIGION**
300 - 399	**SOCIAL SCIENCE** – (Fairy Tales, Fables, Government, Laws)
400 - 499	**LANGUAGE**
500 - 599	**SCIENCE** – (Rocks, Animals, Insects)
600 - 699	**USEFUL ARTS** – (Cooking, Pet Care, Farming)
700 - 799	**FINE ARTS** – (Sports, Arts & Crafts, Photography)
800 - 899	**LITERATURE** – (Poems, Plays, Short Stories, Novels)
900 - 999	**HISTORY** – (Geography, Travel, Biography, History)

THE DEWEY SYSTEM—The 100 Divisions

000	**Generalities**		**500**	**Pure Sciences**
010	Bibliography		510	Mathematics
020	Library & information sciences		520	Astronomy & allied sciences
030	General encyclopedic works		530	Physics
040			540	Chemistry & allied sciences
050	General serial publications		550	Science of earth & other worlds
060	General organizations & museology		560	Paleontology, Paleozoology
070	Journalism, publishing, newspapers		570	Life sciences
080	General collections		580	Botanical sciences
090	Manuscripts & book rarities		590	Zoological sciences
100	**Philosophy**		**600**	**Technology (Applied Sciences)**
110	Metaphysics		610	Medical sciences, Medicine
120	Epistemology, causation, humankind		620	Engineering & allied operations
130	Paranormal phenomena & arts		630	Agriculture & related technologies
140	Specific philosophical viewpoints		640	Home economics & family living
150	Psychology		650	Management & auxiliary services
160	Logic		660	Chemical & related technologies
170	Ethics (Moral philosophy)		670	Manufacturers
180	Ancient, medieval, Oriental		680	Manufacture for specific uses
190	Modern Western philosophy		690	Buildings
200	**Religion**		**700**	**The Arts**
210	Natural religion		710	Civic & landscape art
220	Bible		720	Architecture
230	Christian theology		730	Plastic arts, Sculpture
240	Christian moral & devotional		740	Drawing, decorative & minor arts
250	Local church & religious orders		750	Painting & paintings
260	Social & ecclesiastical theology		760	Graphic arts, Prints
270	History & geography of church		770	Photography & photographs
280	Christian denominations & sects		780	Music
290	Other & comparative religions		790	Recreational & performing arts
300	**Social Sciences**		**800**	**Literature**
310	Statistics		810	American literature in English
320	Political science		820	English & Anglo-Saxon literatures
330	Economics		830	Literature of Germanic languages
340	Law		840	Literature of Romance languages
350	Public administration		850	Italian, Romanian, Rhaeto-Romantic
360	Social problems & services		860	Spanish & Portuguese literature
370	Education		870	Italic literatures, Latin
380	Commerce (Trade)		880	Hellenic literatures, Greek
390	Customs, etiquette, folklore		890	Literatures of other languages
400	**Language**		**900**	**Geography and History**
410	Linguistics		910	General geography, travel
420	English & Anglo-Saxon languages		920	General biography & genealogy
430	Germanic languages, German		930	General history of ancient world
440	Romance languages, French		940	General history of Europe
450	Italian, Romanian, Rhaeto-Romantic		950	General history of Asia
460	Spanish & Portuguese languages		960	General history of Africa
470	Italic languages, Latin		970	General history of North America
480	Hellenic, Classical Greek		980	General history of South America
490	Other languages		990	General history of other areas

Exercise on the Dewey Decimal System. Decide in which one of the ten main Dewey Decimal classes each of the following nonfiction books would be found. Give both the number and the name of the class.

Dewey Decimal Class

_____   1. *Compton's Encyclopedia*

_____   2. *Thanksgiving* by Baldwin

_____   3. *Best-Loved Folktales of the World*

_____   4. *Putting on a Play* by Chalk

_____   5. *Abe Lincoln Grows Up* by Sandburg

_____   6. *Paul Bunyan Swings His Axe* by McCormick

_____   7. *Bible Stories for Children*

_____   8. *Webster's New Students Dictionary*

_____   9. *Space Shuttle* by Hawkes

_____   10. *The American Revolution* by Bliven

_____   11. *The Land and People of Canada* by Ross

_____   12. *Easter Chimes, Stories for Easter and the Spring Season* by Harper

_____   13. *Tigers* by Hunt

_____   14. *Johnny Appleseed and Other Poems* by Lindsay

_____   15. *The World of Dance* by Berger

_____   16. *The Young Photographer* by Craven

_____   17. *Overlord; D-Day and the Invasion of Europe* by Marin

_____   18. *Drawing From Nature* by Arnosky

_____   19. *The Fireside Book of Folk Songs*

_____   20. *What's Cooking? Favorite Recipes From Around the World* by Warner

UNDERSTANDING THE "DECIMAL" IN THE DEWEY DECIMAL SYSTEM

In using the library, you have probably noticed that the class numbers of some books contain decimals (decimal points followed by one or more numbers). This lesson will explain to you why it is necessary to use these numbers and also how books having these numbers should be arranged on the shelf.

You have learned that there are ten main classes in the Dewey Decimal System of Classification. You have also learned that each of the ten main classes is composed of ten divisions. Let's use the 700's, The Arts, as an example. One of the divisions of the 700's is 790—Recreational and Performing Arts. The 790's may be divided into ten sections, as follows:

790   Recreational and Performing Arts
791   Public performances
792   Theater (Stage presentations)
793   Indoor games and amusements
794   Indoor games of skill
795   Games of chance
796   Athletic and outdoor sports and games
797   Aquatic and air sports
798   Equestrian sports and animal racing
799   Fishing, hunting, shooting

Each of the above sections may be expanded as far as necessary by using numbers after a decimal point. The 796 section will serve as our example:

796   Athletic and outdoor sports and games
796.1   Miscellaneous games
796.2   Active games requiring equipment
796.3   Ball games
796.31   Ball thrown or hit by hand—handball, lawn bowling
796.3   Inflated ball thrown or hit by hand—basketball, volleyball
796.33   Inflated ball driven by foot
796.332   American football
796.334   Soccer
796.34   Racket games
796.342   Tennis (lawn tennis)
796.35   Ball driven by club, mallet, bat—including polo, croquet, field hockey, cricket
796.352   Golf
796.357   Baseball

In your mathematics class, the number 796.1 might be read as "seven hundred ninety-six and one tenth." In the library/media center we would say "seven hundred ninety-six point one."

In some mathematics books, decimal numbers are explained like this:

hundreds	tens	ones		tenths	hundreds	thousands
7	9	6	•	3	5	7

This number would be written 796.357, and you might read it as "seven hundred ninety-six and three hundred fifty-seven thousandths." In the Library we would say "seven hundred ninety-six point three five seven."

If we had books with these two class numbers, which would come first on the shelf?

796.3 and 796.31

796.3 is smaller and would come first on the shelf. In shelving library books having decimal numbers, we still follow the principle of the smaller number coming first.

If we had these two numbers, which would come first?

796.358 and 796.4

796.358 is smaller and would come first on the shelf.

Number the following class numbers in the order in which they should be placed on the shelf.

Exercise 1	**Exercise 2**	**Exercise 3**	**Exercise 4**
_____ 621.4	_____ 594	_____ 821	_____ 796.357
_____ 621.3	_____ 595.7	_____ 822.3	_____ 796.33
_____ 621.384	_____ 599	_____ 821.08	_____ 796.35
_____ 621.38	_____ 598.2	_____ 808	_____ 796.54
_____ 621.385	_____ 598.1	_____ 808.81	_____ 796

PUTTING CALL NUMBERS IN ORDER

Number the following call numbers in the order in which you would find them on the shelves in the library/media center. Remember, if two books have the same class number they will be arranged alphabetically by the author's last name (within that number).

Exercise 5	**Exercise 6**	**Exercise 7**
_____ 977.6 F	_____ 301.45 M	_____ 330.973 F
_____ 976.4 B	_____ 301.45 A	_____ 330.9798 H
_____ 977 A	_____ 301.42 J	_____ 330.942 S
_____ 973.7 K	_____ 301.24 B	_____ 331.88 F
_____ 977.6 W	_____ 301.43 L	_____ 331.86 K

Exercise 5	**Exercise 6**	**Exercise 7**
_____ 537.2 B	_____ 629.1309 R	_____ 358.007 E
_____ 537 Y	_____ 629.109 L	_____ 358 L
_____ 537.5 L	_____ 629.13 Z	_____ 358.407 E
_____ 537.2 F	_____ 629.2 T	_____ 358.4 L
_____ 538 T	_____ 629.14 P	_____ 358.417 C

NAME _____

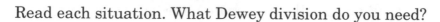

RESEARCH SITUATIONS

Read each situation. What Dewey division do you need?

1. _____ You need a book about butterflies. Where do you look?

2. _____ You need to make a poster for "safety in sports week." You also plan to win the contest for best poster. Where do you look?

3. _____ Your school plans a celebration to mark its 25th anniversary. Where do you find a picture of the sycamore leaf (your school emblem)?

4. _____ Your cousin plans a visit. He knows everything about soccer. Where do you go to "catch up?"

5. _____ Where can you find information about the American colonies?

6. _____ You are starting a new hobby—painting. Where do you look?

7. _____ Where can you find information about famous sports stars?

8. _____ Where can you find help in training your new puppy?

9. _____ Where can you find help in setting up your new aquarium?

10. _____ Where can you find information about black holes in space?

DEWEY SYSTEM— RESEARCH SITUATIONS

Sometimes you will visit your library and ask: Where do I begin to look? What section of the Dewey System do I need to check? How do you decide what section of the Dewey System will help you? You must analyze your research situations. Ask yourself three questions. What do I really need? Where can I find it? And how much information do I need?

Let's look at an example. You are looking for information about space travel and satellites. What do you need? You need information about satellites. Where can you find it? Look at the Dewey chart. The 600–699 section (Useful Arts) has books about transportation including space. Now how much information do you need? You need enough information for a report. So at least two or three books will help.

It is also a good idea to clearly define your research topic. If you are clear about your subject, it will be easier to choose a Dewey section. Let's look at some research situations. See if you can choose a Dewey division to help you.

NAME _____

DEWEY SYSTEM
IN RESEARCH SITUATIONS

Read each situation. What Dewey division do you need?

1. _____ Where can you find help in preparing for a game of hockey?

2. _____ Your teacher read a funny poem. Where can you find more by the same author?

3. _____ Where can you find information about building a bird-house?

4. _____ Where can you find help in learning how to cook?

5. _____ Your new neighbors are always gardening. Where can you find information about gardening?

6. _____ Your class will be putting on a play. Where do you look to find a "good one?"

7. _____ Where can you find a recipe for chocolate cookies?

8. _____ Your teacher plans a unit on ancient Egypt. Where can you find information about the pyramids?

9. _____ Your little sister wants you to read her a fairy tale. Where do you look to find one?

10. _____ Where can you find information about space travel?

NAME _____

RESEARCH SITUATIONS:
WHAT DIVISION DO YOU NEED?

Read each situation. Choose a division. Write the Dewey number and subject.

1. _____ _____ You need a book about sports. You aren't certain if you will join the soccer or baseball team. Name the division.

2. _____ _____ You need a book about the lives of famous people. You need to write about a famous person for your report. Name the division.

3. _____ _____ You are checking about the traditions and customs of Ireland. Name the division.

4. _____ _____ You are looking for a fairy tale to read to your younger cousin. Name the division.

5. _____ _____ You need a book that will teach you Spanish so that you can talk to the new student in class. Name the division.

6. _____ _____ You need a book about baking cookies for a school party. You volunteered to bake a batch. Name the division.

7. _____ _____ You are doing a report about the American colonies. Name the division.

8. _____ _____ Your parents plan to travel to Maine. You are going too! But you need to know what type of clothes to wear. Name the division.

9. _____ _____ Your new neighbors are Hindu. But you know nothing about this religion. Where can you find more information?

10. _____ _____ Whales and sharks. Where can you find more information? Name the division.

NAME _____

WHAT DEWEY SUBJECT DIVISION?

Read each title or subject below. In what Dewey division would you find it? You may check the chart.

Subjects

1. _____ Rocks

2. _____ Stars

3. _____ Sea Animals

4. _____ Coral

5. _____ Whales

6. _____ Cooking

7. _____ Sports

8. _____ History

9. _____ Drawing

10. _____ Biography

Titles

1. _____ *Learning French*

2. _____ *Making Costumes*

3. _____ *The Pioneers*

4. _____ *Life in the American Colonies*

5. _____ *Whales and Other Sea Animals*

6. _____ *The Romans*

7. _____ *Soccer!*

8. _____ *Learning Spanish*

9. _____ *Sports in America*

10. _____ *Explorers in America*

USING THE CARD CATALOG— CHOOSING A CARD

You need information quickly and you want to find it easily. How do you find what you want? Use the card catalog. You already know that the card catalog is divided into three sections. You can find a card for every book in your library under a title, subject, or author.

The information is the same on these cards. But notice the first line of these cards is different. An author card begins with the author's name. A title card begins with the title. And the subject card begins with the subject written in capital letters. What information can you find on a catalog card? Let's review:

---

(1) 973   (2)   History of New Jersey

    St   (3)   Roger State.   (4)   Rockville, New Jersey

             (5)   State Press,   (6)   1989.

             (7)   This is the complete history of New Jersey.

             (8)   1. New Jersey   I. Author   II. Subject

---

1. Call number— tells you where you can find the book in your library.

2. Book title

3. Author

4. Place of publication

5. Publishers

6. Copyright date

7. Summary of the book

8. Tracing—other places in the card catalog where you can find this book.

NAME _____

COMPARING CARDS

The Planets

Z   Solar, Jason.

567   The Planets /

So   Jason Solar—Startown, N.Y.: Galaxy Press, 1989.

         xiv, 323 p. ; 25 cm.—(Tells about the planets in the solar

system)

         1. Planets   I. Author   II. Subject.

STARS, GALAXIES AND THE PLANETS

Z   System, Peter.

567   Stars, Galaxies and the Planets /

Sy   Peter System—Milky Way Town, N.Y.: Milky Way Press, 1987.

         xiv, 118 p. ; 18 cm.—(Tells about stars, galaxies, and planets)

         1. Planets   I. Author   II. Subject

---

1. _____   What are the call numbers?

2. _____   Which book is the newest?

3. _____   Name the publisher of each book.

4. _____   What is the call number of *The Planets?*

5. _____   What book was published in Milky Way Town, NY?

6. _____   Under which subject will you find these books?

7. _____   Who is the author of *The Planets*?

8. _____   Who is the author of *Stars, Galaxies, and the Planets?*

9. _____   Where was *The Planets* published?

10. _____   In which state were both books published?

COMPARING CATALOG CARDS

	History of the U.S.A.	
Z	State, Emily.	
973	History of the U.S.A. /	
St	Emily State—Maptown, Washington: Historical Press, 1989.	
	xiv, 240 p. ; 25 cm.—(Gives a summary of U.S. history)	
	1. History, U.S. I. Author II. Subject	

	History of the United States: 1776–1876.	
Z	Country, Richard.	
973	History of the United States: 1776–1876 /	
Co	Richard Country—Historyville, Washington:History Press, 1987.	
	xx, 96 p. ; 15 cm,—(History of U.S. from 1776–1876)	
	1. History I. Author II. Subject	

1. _____ Which book will give you information about when our country was the youngest?

2. _____ Which book is the newest?

3. _____ Name the publisher of each book.

4. _____ What is the call number of each book?

5. _____ Which book was published in Maptown, Washington?

6. _____ What subject will you find in these books?

7. _____ Who is the author of *History of the U.S.A.*?

8. _____ Who is the author of *History of the United States:1776–1876*?

9. _____ Where was the *History of the U.S.A.* made?

10. _____ In which state were both books published?

NAME _____

COMPARING CATALOG CARDS—OVERVIEW

	Insects that Crawl From My Closet
F	Wing, Robert.
	Insects that Crawl From My Closet /
Wi	Robert Wing—Dustyville, New York: Dark Press, 1989.
	x, 96 p. ; 10 cm.—(A story of a strange day)
	1. Fiction—Insects I. Author II. Subject

	The Day the Cat Ate My Pajamas
F	Roberts, Gretchun.
Ro	The Day the Cat Ate My Pajamas /
	Gretchun Roberts—Meow, New York: Cat Time Press, 1987.
	x, 96 p. ; 10 cm.—(Story of a strange cat)
	1. Fiction—Cats I. Author II. Subject

---

1. _____   What book is about a cat?

2. _____   What book is the newest?

3. _____   Name the publisher of each book.

4. _____   What is the call number of each book?

5. _____   What book was published in Meow, NY?

6. _____   Under what subject will you find these books?

7. _____   Who is the author of *The Day the Cat Ate My Pajamas?*

8. _____   Who is the author of *Insects that Crawl From My Closet?*

9. _____   Where was *Insects That Crawl From My Closet* published?

10. _____   In what state were both books published?

CARD CATALOG— RESEARCH SITUATIONS

How do you decide what catalog card you need? When you are faced with a research situation, it is important to get the facts first. Do you need an author, title, or subject card? Ask yourself: do you have the author's name? Or do you have the title of the book? Or do you have the subject?

Let's look at a typical research situation. Your teacher assigned a report about science experiments and weather. Do you have the author's name? Do you need the title of the book? No. Do you have the subjects? Yes. You can look under science experiments or weather.

Let's look at another situation. You need to know if Arthur Small wrote twenty-seven mystery books. Do you have the titles? No. Do you have the author's name? Yes. Do you have the subject? Yes. Mystery. So where do you check? Use your card catalog. You could check mystery. But then you would have to check if there were twenty-seven cards by the same author. And you would have to check the entire mystery drawer. Or you could check the author's name.

Check under the author's name. It will be easier.

Now let's look at some research situations.

WHAT CATALOG CARD DO YOU NEED?

Read each research situation. Do you need a subject, author, or title card? Give the title, author, or subject for each situation.

1. _____ You are studying the stars. You have been watching a really big one from your window. What card do you need?

2. _____ You are making a poster for the science fair. You plan to draw the different types of clouds. Where do you look?

3. _____ Did Marsh Day really write twenty-seven books about ants?

4. _____ You need a book about George Washington.

5. _____ Did Reba MacIntire write a mystery called *The Strange Tree?*

6. _____ Are there any books about the stars?

7. _____ Are there any books about Sally Ride?

8. _____ Your dog needs training where do you look?

9. _____ Are there any books about Peter Starr?

10. _____ You are making a poster for good nutrition month. You plan to win the poster contest. Where can you find information about nutrition and cooking?

NAME _____

RESEARCH SITUATIONS:
WHAT CATALOG CARD DO YOU NEED?

Read each research situation. Decide which card will help you and then write "author," "title," or "subject" on the first blank. Write the *actual* author name, title, or subject heading on the second blank.

1. _____ _____ You are collecting information about how people live in Greece for a report.

2. _____ _____ You need to know about safety rules for skateboarding.

3. _____ _____ Roger Scott wrote five books about hamsters. Does your library have any of them?

4. _____ _____ You are getting braces. Your friend just read a good book called *Orthodontics and You*. You want to check the book out.

5. _____ _____ You are doing a report about the Roman Army for extra credit.

6. _____ _____ There are twenty-three students in your class. Your teacher assigned a report about explorers. Will your library have enough books for all?

7. _____ _____ Myna Bruet wrote *Hamsters, Gerbils, and Mice*. It's one of a series. Does your library have the entire set?

8. _____ _____ You are entering a cookie contest. You need a super recipe.

9. _____ _____ Your cousin is coming and he knows all the rules of soccer. Where do you find the official rules?

10. _____ _____ You are writing a report about submarines. Are there any books about submarines written by Robert Sub?

NAME _____

RESEARCH SITUATIONS:
WHAT CATALOG CARD DO YOU NEED?

Read each research situation. Decide which card will help you and then write "author," "title," or "subject" on the blank.

1. _____ Did Roger Peterson write a mystery book called *Green Tree*?

2. _____ Are there any books about hamsters?

3. _____ Are there any books about rocks and minerals?

4. _____ Are there any books about boats?

5. _____ Did Peter Johnson write a book called *Over the Mountain*?

6. _____ Are there enough books about ants in the library for everyone to check one out? (There are 23 students.)

7. _____ Did Roger Ant write *All About Ants*?

8. _____ Are there any books about space in your library?

9. _____ Is *Green Fire* in your library?

10. _____ Did John James write a fairy tale called *Peter Bunkins*?

NAME _____

NAME THAT CARD

Read each question. Do you need an author, subject, or title card?

1. *History of Toys* _____

2. TOYS _____

3. Alfred B. Toy _____

4. *Cooking for Kids* _____

5. Alfred B. Cook _____

6. COOKING _____

7. *Indians of the West* _____

8. Arthur C. Indian _____

9. INDIANS _____

10. *Goldfish and Other Pets* _____

11. ROCKS AND MINERALS _____

12. *Stories for Young* _____

13. Jerome C. Johnson _____

14. *How to Raise Your Gerbil* _____

15. GERBILS _____

16. *Arthur C. Gerbil* _____

17. KITES _____

18. Arthur James Kite _____

19. BOX KITES _____

20. *History of the Kite* _____

NAME _____

CHOOSE YOUR CARD

Catalog card situations. Read the titles, authors, and subjects below. Identify them as title, author, or subject. Remember, the subject is written in capital letters.

1. *The History of the American Colonies* _____

2. J.J. HOOK _____

3. *Crabs of the Sea* _____

4. TIGERS _____

5. *Tigers in the Wild* _____

6. *Shipbuilding in the Navy* _____

7. *Cats and their Habits* _____

8. CATS _____

9. Richard Cat _____

10. CARS _____

11. *Kites: How to Fly Them* _____

12. *The Blue Rabbit* _____

13. *Horses in America* _____

14. KITES _____

15. Roger Horse _____

16. *The Mouse in the Cheese Factory* _____

17. MICE _____

18. *The Green Leaf Mystery* _____

19. Richard Mice _____

20. Richard Greenleaf _____

COMPARING ENCYCLOPEDIA INDEXES

Each encyclopedia has one volume that lists the articles in the encyclopedia alphabetically. This volume is called an *index*. Use the index to find the information you need quickly. Remember, you will not find the same information in every encyclopedia. So compare encyclopedia indexes when you are collecting your research.

Let's look at two indexes about the same subject.

Gardening

flowers	F– 501
plants	P– 605
seeds, types	S– 315
soil, potting	S– 311
	Encyclopedia of Plants

Gardening

flowers, types	F– 301
flowers, when to cut	F– 306
gardening tools	G– 317
how to buy seeds	S– 301
	Plant Encyclopedia

Do each of these encyclopedias have the same information? No, they do not. What encyclopedia has information about tools? Check the *Plant Encyclopedia*. Where can you find information about potting soil? Check the *Encyclopedia of Plants*.

NAME _____

COMPARING ENCYCLOPEDIA INDEXES—
TRANSPORTATION

Transportation	
Automobile	A–61
Busses	B–3
Cars	C–81
Helicopters	H–91
Submarines	S–135
Trains	T–147
Trolley cars	T–189

Encyclopedia of Transportation

Transportation	
Automobiles	A–36
Airplanes	A–89
Antique Cars	A–91
Balloons, Hot Air	B–367
Boats	B–411
Jets	J–502
Sailboats	S–496
Speedboats	S–431

Encyclopedia of Travel

Read each index. Answer questions.

1. _____ Where can you find information about sailboats?

2. _____ Can you find information about trolley cars in both indexes?

3. _____ On what page can you find information about submarines?

4. _____ On what page can you find information about airplanes?

5. _____ Can you find information about helicopters in both indexes?

6. _____ What type of boats can you find information about?

7. _____ Is there any information about antique cars?

8. _____ Are there two entries for automobiles?

9. _____ Can you find information about hot air balloons?

10. _____ Can you find information about jets in both indexes?

COMPARING ENCYCLOPEDIA INDEXES
HOBBIES

HOBBIES
Arts and Crafts	A–305
Basketball	B–401
Coins, Collecting	C-275
Dancing	D–117
Dolls, Collecting	D–87
Football	F–301
Hockey	H–565
Karate	K–411
Stamps, Collecting	S–329

Encyclopedia of the World

HOBBIES
Baseball	B–367
Chess	C–63
Drawing	D–17
Ice Hockey	I–309
Judo	J–287
Painting	P–111
Swimming	S–117
Water Sports	W–294

Encyclopedia of Knowledge

Read each index. Compare. Answer these questions.

1. _____ Where would you find information about collecting stamps?

2. _____ What encyclopedia has information about karate?

3. _____ Can you find information about chess in both indexes?

4. _____ Can you find information about water sports in both indexes?

5. _____ Is there any information about hockey?

6. _____ Is there information about basketball?

7. _____ Is there information about ice hockey?

8. _____ What are the names of the entries about art?

9. _____ Where can you find information about swimming?

10. _____ Can you find information about drawing in both indexes?

USING A MAGAZINE GUIDE

Do you need information from a magazine? How do you get the information that you want quickly and easily? You can use a magazine guide. A magazine guide works like an index. Let's look at a sample.

Hobbies.	"All About Baseball " .<u>Sports Digest.</u> Oct 15, 1989.
	"Better Soccer Playing" . <u>Sports Digest.</u> Sept. 16, 1987.
	"Hockey Stars" .<u>Hockey Digest.</u> July 23, 1989.

If you need information about famous players of hockey, what article might help? Check "Hockey Stars" in *Hockey Digest* (July 23, 1989). Do you see how using a magazine guide will cut your research time? It saves you much time in looking through the many magazines that your library has.

Remember, the magazine guide may not index the magazine you are looking for. So always check the magazine guide to see what magazines are indexed. This will give you a better idea of what information you can expect to find.

INTRODUCTION TO RESEARCH

Being able to research a topic is a skill you can use, not only in future classes at school, but also as you become interested in topics in your everyday life.

Research can be fun and is nothing to be afraid of. When you have a topic in mind and you are ready to go find information in the library, think of your research as a treasure hunt—looking in many places to find all the information you need. Along the way you will discover many valuable books, magazines, reference books, and other materials that you probably never knew existed.

When you've collected your materials, have taken notes, and are ready to write, don't think of your report as a terrible task—this is an opportunity for you to share with others the information that you've discovered. Your report is a chance to say something about a topic in your own way, with your own creative angle, and including supportive details that you think are especially interesting and worth sharing.

When you write a paper based on research you have done, you have to make sure that your information has order and can be understood by someone who has not done all the research you have. If you take the time to carefully gather your information, organize it, and write your paper, you should have a great report that others will enjoy reading.

Although writing a report requires a lot of work that is not always easy, you are learning on your very own, outside of the classroom. You can be proud that when you finish your research, your report reflects information that you yourself have gathered and organized. You have taught yourself and you should feel good about the work you've done.

BRAINSTORMING

After you are assigned a category for your report (rarely will your teacher require you to think up your own category with no guidelines) you need to pick an aspect of the category and brainstorm.

When you brainstorm you ask yourself questions about the topic you have chosen—questions you are particularly curious about. But you don't have to write down questions, you can write phrases, words, or whatever comes to your mind when you think about your topic. Let your thoughts run free to generate ideas. Don't worry about organization. Ask yourself "What do I know about this topic?" and "What do I *want* to know about this topic?"

Pretend that your teacher tells the class that each person will have to write a report on WEATHER. Clearly, the topic "weather" is too broad to do a report on—you must narrow this category down to something that interests you. You have always been fascinated with violent storms and what makes them happen. But the category "violent storms" is still too broad. You could write about tornadoes, typhoons, hailstorms, floods, blizzards, how about a hurricane? Your grandmother lives in South Carolina and has been in a hurricane—maybe you could call and ask her more about what a hurricane is like in real life.

Below is an example of a "Brainstorm Idea Page." Use this as a model to begin your own brainstorming process. Remember: Don't worry about spelling, punctuation, or putting your thoughts in a special order. Just write, write, write!

Brainstorm Idea Page

HURRICANE

Prevention?	Conditions for	Protection
Time of year?	Movement over sea	human deaths/year
Speed?	Worst?	Why?
Only over water?	shelters?	Eye of
Where most frequent?	Last how long?	How different from typhoon?
Like tornado?	Predicting	I should interview grandma in SC.

Why do they have names?—Other storms don't

CHOOSING YOUR TOPIC

Before you begin your research you must choose a topic. Often your teacher will give you a category and you are able to pick a topic that falls into this category. If you can choose a topic that interests you, you will probably do a better job and have more fun writing your report. Even if you *are* given a specific topic, *you* are still writing the report and what you write is your choice. Even if you and all your classmates have the same topic you will have a different interest in the topic and different questions about a specific aspect of the topic. Some of the facts you decide to include in your report will be the same as your classmates', but your report will include details that are most interesting to you, and what *you* write most about will make your report your own.

For example, if you are to write on the Navajo Indian tribe, depending on what interests you, you could title your paper NAVAJO FOLKLORE & CUSTOMS, GREAT NAVAJO CHIEFS, HISTORICAL EVENTS OF THE NAVAJO TRIBE, NAVAJO ARTS & CRAFTS—the possibilities are endless, even if you are given a topic as specific as "the Navajo Indian tribe"!

When you are choosing your topic you also need to consider the length of your report. If your teacher wants one or two pages, you will need to have a narrower topic than if he/she wants a 3–5 page report. You will also do a different amount and type of research depending on the length of your assigned report. Generally, a narrower topic will help you focus your research and make the writing of your paper easier.

Be careful not to make your topic *too* narrow. If your topic is too specific, you may not be able to come up with enough information to write your report.

Look at the following topics. In this case the teacher wanted the class to do a report on an aspect of American history. How about:

THE AMERICAN REVOLUTION
(too broad of a topic)

PAUL REVERE'S LIGHT IN THE OLD NORTH CHURCH
(too specific)

PAUL REVERE'S ROLE IN THE AMERICAN REVOLUTION
(better)

NAME _____

CHOOSING TOPICS

Read the following sets of research topics. Write "broad" if the topic is too general. Write "specific" if the topic is too narrow. Write "good" if the topic would work for a report *(Hint: You will use all three answers in each set.)*

1. a the Solar System   _____
    b Jupiter's Colors   _____
    c the Planet Jupiter   _____

2. a Sir Francis Drake's Boat   _____
    b Explorers   _____
    c Sir Francis Drake   _____

3. a Taking Care of Your Dog   _____
    b Feeding Your Dog   _____
    c Raising Pets   _____

4. a Indian Tribes of North America   _____
    b the Arapaho Indians   _____
    c Arapaho Indian Tools   _____

5. a the History of Baseball   _____
    b Babe Ruth   _____
    c the Role of the First Baseman in Baseball   _____

6. a Cooking Around the World   _____
    b French Cheeses—How Are They Made?   _____
    c French Toast   _____

7. a the King Cobra   _____
    b Snakes   _____
    c the Snake's Digestive System   _____

8. a How a Sailboat Works   _____
    b a Boat's Rudder   _____
    c Boats   _____

CHOOSING TOPICS

Read the following sets of research topics. Write "broad" if the topic is too general. Write "specific" if the topic is too narrow. Write "good" if the topic would work for a report *(Hint: You will use all three answers in each set.)*

1. a Black Death   _____
    b Treatment of Black Death   _____
    c the Middle Ages   _____

2. a Cowboys: Saddles & Equipment   _____
    b Cowboys   _____
    c the Rodeo   _____

3. a Life in Quebec   _____
    b Life in Canada   _____
    c Food in Quebec   _____

4. a a Plant's Roots   _____
    b Parts of the Plant   _____
    c Plants   _____

5. a the Victorian Music Hall   _____
    b Victorian Entertainment   _____
    c the Victorian Age   _____

6. a Prehistoric Weapons   _____
    b Weapons   _____
    c the Samurai Dagger   _____

7. a Caves   _____
    b How Caves Form   _____
    c Stalagmites   _____

GETTING READY FOR RESEARCH

Before you get started with your research, you should know about some of the items, or "tools" that will make your research easier and help keep you organized.

Folder: A folder is handy to keep your research notes, photocopies from the library, and any handouts your teacher or librarian gives you. Using a folder also makes it easy to transport your research materials from home to school and to the library. Be sure to label the folder with your project name; and your own name, address, and phone number.

Note cards (3 x 5 and 4 x 6): Note cards are easier to use than a notebook when writing a research report because they can be rearranged and reordered when it comes time to lay out your notes and begin actually writing the report. This process will make more sense to you when you start your research. You will write your notes on the larger note cards and you will keep track of your sources (encyclopedias, books, magazines, etc.) on the smaller note cards.

Large Envelopes & Rubberbands: Since note cards are smaller than a notebook and are not bound together, it is a good idea to put a rubberband around each set of note cards and put both packs of cards in a large envelope for safekeeping.

Thesaurus: When you actually start writing your paper, you may find it difficult to find different ways of expressing what you have read in a book. Using a variety of words to write your paper will also make the report interesting for the reader.

Dictionary: Undoubtedly you will come across several words you do not know while you are researching your topic. Learning new vocabulary is an extra benefit you get from writing a research paper! On the following page you will see a "dictionary bank." Add to this bank whenever you come to a word you do not know in your reading. Refer back to the bank when you start writing your report—perhaps you can use one of the new words you learned.

Research materials: Of course you will need the source to write your report. You should probably plan to use an encyclopedia, two or three books, and one or two magazines, plus any other materials such as an almanac, a biographical dictionary, and material from the vertical file—depending on your report. All of these sources will be discussed further on page 38.

DICTIONARY BANK

New Words   Definitions

1. _____

2. _____

3. _____

4. _____

5. _____

6. _____

7. _____

8. _____

9. _____

10. _____

CHOOSING SOURCES

Now that you have your research topic, you need to collect sources of information on your topic. There are so many to choose from in the library. So what do you do? Decide how much material you need. Are you writing a one-page report, a five-page report, or only a paragraph? It will make a difference in what type and how many research sources you choose.

Although the length and topic of your report will limit you, to some degree, on how many and what type of resources you will use, you should at least be familiar with the types of materials that your library has to offer. Below you will find a descriptive guide of informational sources that will help you choose the types of materials you need to write your report. (You will probably already know how to use some of the materials, the other, less familiar resources will be explained further on the pages following.)

Encyclopedia: The encyclopedia, or encyclopedia index rather, is perhaps the first place you should go to get a broad overview of your topic and to decide exactly which aspects of your topic that you may want to cover. The encyclopedia will give you basic facts about your topic, but it will not give you many interesting details that will give your report color and life.

If you only use an encyclopedia for your report, not only will your teacher be able to tell, but your report will not be very interesting. You should also keep in mind that the more specific your topic is, the less likely that the encyclopedia will have any information on it. (For example, the encyclopedia probably has several pages on DOGS, but if your report is on a special *breed* of dog, you will find little, if any, information on the specific breed in the encyclopedia.

When you use an encyclopedia remember:

- Look in the index first under your topic name. The index may list another heading that has information on your topic.

- Look at the end of the encyclopedia article you use to find **cross-references**—a list of other headings that may have further information that might be useful to you.

Books: If you look up one book in the card catalog and go to it, you will likely find many more books in the same area that will be helpful to you—thanks to the Dewey Decimal System.

When you use books to find information you should go through several to see which ones will be the most helpful to you. The easiest way to do this is to check the book's table of contents to see if your topic might be listed as a main heading or chapter. Check the index as well to see exactly which pages contain the information you need.

Magazines: Magazines are sometimes called **periodicals** because, unlike books, magazines come out on a schedule periodically—every week, two weeks, month, or quarter of the year. Magazines are valuable because they carry current information that may not be available in books yet.

How do you know where to find the articles on your topic? The *Reader's Guide to Periodical Literature* is a huge index that lists the magazines (and page numbers) that contain information on specific topics. All you need to do is look up your topic name (as you would in an encyclopedia index) and the *Reader's Guide* will tell you the dates and titles of the magazines and magazine articles that feature the information you're looking for.

NAME _____

THE READER'S GUIDE TO PERIODICAL LITERATURE

Your teacher will give each of you a topic. Using the *Reader's Guide*, look up three magazine articles and record the following information below:

Subject: _____

1. Article title _____

    Author _____

    Magazine _____

    Volume _____ Pages _____

    Date _____ Pictures? _____

2. Article title _____

    Author _____

    Magazine _____

    Volume _____ Pages _____

    Date _____ Pictures? _____

3. Article title _____

    Author _____

    Magazine _____

    Volume _____ Pages _____

    Date _____ Pictures? _____

USING A MAGAZINE GUIDE—TOYS

A History of American Toys. <u>History Magazine</u>. Oct 27, 1987.

A History of the Teddy Bear. <u>History Magazine</u>. Nov 3, 1989.

How to Make a Dollhouse. <u>Activities for Children</u>. Apr 13, 1987.

How to Make Simple Toys. <u>Arts and Crafts</u>. Apr 3, 1986.

Marbles. <u>Play and Children</u>. May 13, 1989.

Toys for Holidays. <u>Games and Children</u>. May 13, 1989.

Toys for Young People. <u>Toy Magazine</u>. Sept 3, 1987.

Trains. <u>Young People's Magazine</u>. May 3, 1988.

Young People's Dolls. <u>Toy Magazine</u>. Oct 31, 1989.

Read the index. What article will help you?

1. How did the teddy bear get its name? _____

2. What was the first china doll made of? _____

3. Are blocks a good toy to give young people? _____

4. What type of toy can you make easily? _____

5. What toy makes a good gift? _____

6. Why are trains so popular with young people? _____

7. What type of toys did the colonists have? _____

8. What is a cat's eye marble? _____

9. Are stuffed toys safe? _____

10. Can you make a doll house with only a few tools?_____

NAME _____

USING A MAGAZINE GUIDE—COOKING

Cooking

Baking for Kids. Cooking Magazine. Oct 11, 1987.

Cookies for Holidays. Cookie Digest. Oct 27, 1987.

Cakes for Special Occasions. Cooking Digest. Dec 19, 1989.

Cooking and Nutrition. Health Magazine. Sept 21, 1989.

Decorating Cakes. Cooking Digest. Oct 20, 1987.

Making Dinner. Health Magazine. March 20, 1989.

Making Lunch. Health Magazine. May 19, 1986.

Making Salads. Health Magazine. Oct 13, 1989.

Making Soups. Health Magazine. April 13, 1987.

Vitamins and Cooking. Health Magazine. Nov 21, 1989.

Read the index. What article will help you?

1. Where would you find help to bake a cake for your sister's birthday?

    _____

2. Is it a good idea to mix rice and beans to make a nutritious dish? What article
    will help you? _____

3. How does cooking your food affect its vitamins? _____

4. Help! You need tips on decorating the cake you just made. _____

5. Are there any good recipes for baking that are just for kids?

    _____

6. How do you make a good salad? _____

7. You need a special recipe for dinner. _____

8. You need a cookie recipe for a school party. _____

9. What article is written just for kids? _____

10. What two articles will help you with nutrition? _____

    _____

USING A MAGAZINE GUIDE

<u>Hobbies</u>

All About Baseball. <u>Sports Digest.</u> Oct 15, 1987.

All About Chess. <u>Hobby Magazine</u>. May 6, 1989.

Baseball Card Collecting. <u>Hobby Magazine</u>. May 19, 1987.

Coin Collecting. <u>Hobby Digest</u>. August 3, 1989.

Dolls: Making Clothes. <u>Hobby Digest</u>. Nov 19, 1987.

Football for Teens. <u>Sports Digest</u>. July 13, 1989.

Painting for Kids. <u>Arts and Crafts Magazine</u>. Apr 17, 1987.

Stamp Collecting. <u>Hobby Digest</u>. Apr 7, 1987.

Stamps of the World: Building Your Collection. <u>Stamp World</u>. June 16, 1989.

Water Color Painting for Young People. <u>Arts and Crafts</u>. Apr 17, 1989.

Read the magazine guide. Answer these questions.

1. Where can you find information about collecting baseball cards?

   _____

2. You found a stamp on an old envelope. What article may help you find what country it comes from? _____

3. Where can you find information about football? _____

4. Your uncle plays chess. You don't. What article might help? _____

5. What two articles will tell you about painting? _____

   _____

6. What article will help you make a new set of doll clothes?

   _____

7. You need more information about baseball. _____

8. Your cousin collects coins. What article will give you more information?

   _____

9. What article was written for young people about football? _____

10. What two articles are about stamps? _____

    _____

USING A BOOK INDEX

A book index is an alphabetized list of subjects. Page numbers follow the subjects so that you can find information quickly and easily. The index is much more detailed than a table of contents. If you need *general* information, choose a table of contents. If you need *specific* information, choose an index. For example, let's say that you need information about ants. What would you choose? Choose the table of contents. This is a general question. But let's say that you need to know about brown ants. Where would you check? Choose the index. This is a specific question.

Let's look at part of an index.

> apples, types, 31
>
> fruit (a chart of common seeds), 25
>
> grapes, 3
>
> honeydew melons, 13
>
> iceberg lettuce, 7
>
> lemons, 37

On what page will you find information about apples and their types? On page 31.

Where will you find a chart showing the different seeds of common fruits? On page 25.

Use a book index to find information easily and quickly.

BOOK INDEXES—COOKING

Cooking	
baking	3
buying your ingredients	47
cake	81
cookies	31
ingredients, measuring	46
mixing	27
oven, using the	17
pans	79
pots	80
preparing your recipe	33
reading your recipes	37
recipes	35
utensils, baking	91

Read the index. Answer the questions.

1. What page will tell you how to read your recipe? _____

2. How do you shop for ingredients? _____

3. What pots should you use? _____

4. How do you measure correctly? _____

5. How do you make cookies? _____

6. How do you set the oven? _____

7. How do you select pans? _____

8. How do you mix ingredients correctly? _____

9. Where can you find information about cakes? _____

10. Where can you find information about recipes? _____

NAME _____

BOOK INDEXES—TERMITES

body parts	36
enemies	29
flying ants	3
homes	2
how to know if you have termites	129
insects they are related to	93
nests	17
types	29
what they eat	87
when you find them	17

Read the index. Answer the questions.

1. How do you know if your house has termites? _____

2. Do termites really eat wood? _____

3. Are ants related to termites? _____

4. Are ladybugs and termites friends? _____

5. How many legs does a termite have? _____

6. Is flying ant another name for termite? _____

7. What do termites eat? _____

8. Do termites live in wood? _____

9. Are spiders related to termites? _____

10. Can you find termites in the dark? _____

BOOK INDEXES—TOYS

Toys	
American toys	3
history	31
homemade toys	57
houses, doll	33
how to make simple toys	167
teddy bears	89
toys for young people	183
toys that fly	79
trains	121
types	111

Read the index. Answer these questions.

1. Where will you find information about the teddy bear? _____

2. Is a kite a simple toy?   _____

3. When was the first train made?   _____

4. What are easy toys that you can make?   _____

5. What are common toys for children?   _____

6. What materials do you need to make a doll house? _____

7. What type of toys did the colonists play with?   _____

8. Did the children of the wild west have toys?   _____

9. When and where was the first train made?   _____

10. Can kites that fly be made at home?   _____

ALMANAC

When is Robert E. Lee's birthday? Who is the current governor of Tennessee? Who was the first person to reach the South Pole? Where was Andrew Jackson born? How many recognized dog breeds are there? How wide is Nebraska? The almanac is a reference book full of odd and unusual facts that is published once a year. However, it also contains statistics and facts from previous years. If you need specific information that is more recent than what can be found in books or encyclopedias, the almanac can help you. Often times trivial but interesting facts can liven up a research report if the information is presented appropriately.

Since an almanac is not organized in alphabetical order, you need to know the key word of the information you're looking for so that you can use the index to look up the fact you need. In an almanac the index is located in the *front* of the book where the key words (subject headings) are listed alphabetically. The main subject headings are in bold face type. The subheadings (related to the main headings) are indented under the main headings.

Look at the example questions below. The key word is underlined—this is the heading name you would look under in the almanac's index to answer the question.

When is United Nations Day?

Who was Miss America in 1962?

In what city is the Cotton Bowl located?

What are the principal gases in the earth's atmosphere?

Where were the Winter Olympics held in 1976?

How many people work for the postal service?

Who was the first person in space?

Where can you find information on television awards?

When is Citizenship Day?

How much does the Liberty Bell weigh?

What is the world's longest river?

USING THE ALMANAC

An almanac is a collection of facts and statistics that is published yearly. These facts cover many different subjects. An almanac is an excellent research tool. You may find valuable information for your research report.

What type of subjects will you find in an almanac? You can find information about the solar system and the planets. Such facts as how far the planets are from the earth can be found. Facts about the constellations. Facts about the weather. The history of the United States. Facts about countries. Facts about television. Facts about awards. Facts about the presidents. You name it, the almanac might just have it.

Let's say that you are writing a report about Saturn. You have just collected information from magazines, books, and the encyclopedia. Can you find any information in an almanac? Yes, check the table of contents. You will see that a summary of the basic facts of each planet is presented. Now you can begin your research.

And how do you collect this research? Learn how to use the table of contents of the almanac. It is so detailed, you might really call it the index.

Let's work with the almanac.

USING THE ALMANAC

Read this part of an almanac. Answer the following research questions.

Baseball—	
Addresses of teams	820
All Star games	865
All-Time leaders	881
Batting Records	869–880
Home Runs	868
Little League Series	876
Pitching Records	870,874
World Series	877
Space Developments—	
Apollo Trips	168–169
Astronauts	169–170
Cosmonauts	168–169
First person in space	168
First space walk	168
Mars Landing	484
Moonwalk, U.S.	169, 482
Space Shuttle	170,486
Television—	
Actors, Actresses	399–415
Awards	350–359
Favorite U.S. Programs	372, 373
Sets, number of	373
Time Spent Viewing	372
Video Cassette Recorders	97

On what pages will you find answers to these questions.

1. How many televisions sets in the U.S.?   _____

2. What is the average time Americans spend watching television?

                                                              _____

3. Who was part of the space shuttle Discovery crew? _____

4. Who was the first person in space?   _____

5. Who was the first American in space?   _____

6. What is the address of the Los Angeles Dodgers? _____

7. Who hit the most home runs in 1986?   _____

8. What was the score of the All Star Game in 1986? _____

9. Where can you find information about television awards? _____

10. How many video cassette recorders are in the U.S.? _____

USING THE ALMANAC—OVERVIEW

Read these parts of the almanac. Answer the following questions.

Animals

Cat Breeds	156
Collection of Animal Names	154
Endangered Species	153
Farm Animals	154
Major Poisonous Animals	155
Speed of Animals	154
Wildlife Animals	149
Zoo Animals	156

Americans

Actors	399–415
Artists	388–390
Athletes	856–858
Authors	379
Cartoonists	354
Rock and Roll Musicians	398–399
Scientists	377–394

Television

Top Television Programs	373
Sports Programs	820–821
T.V. Networks	373

On which pages will you find answers to these questions?

1. Is the giant panda on the endangered species list? _____

2. Is it true that the cheetah runs 70 m.p.h.? _____

3. Is it true that the stingray is a poisonous animal? _____

4. How many zoos are in the U.S.? _____

5. Is the ocelot on the endangered species list? _____

6. How many animals are in the Bronx Zoo? _____

7. How many cat breeds are there? _____

8. Is *band* the name of a collection of gorillas? _____

9. Is the gila monster a poisonous lizard? _____

10. Is it true the poisonous rattlesnake is 2–8 feet long? _____

11. Is the muppet show one of the top ten television programs? _____

12. Were the Super Bowl games ever on the list of top ten television programs?

_____

ATLAS

If you are researching a *place* for your report, such as a continent, a foreign country or city, or even a body of water, the atlas is definitely a resource you should look into. Although you may say "But the atlas is just a book of maps," these maps will give you populations, climates, crops, weather systems, resources and products, and any physical information about a place that you would ever need to know. Atlases are especially fun to use because there is very little reading involved—all of the information is placed before you in picture form on maps.

BIOGRAPHICAL DICTIONARY

If you are researching a *person* for your report, you can use the biographical dictionary to look up basic facts about the person (much like you would use the encyclopedia—for an overview). By reading the entry on the person you are researching you will likely get more ideas about what you want to write about in your report and what resources you can look up next.

VERTICAL FILE

Most libraries have some sort of filing system that is arranged alphabetically by subject. All of the subjects categorized have their own file folder containing articles, pamphlets, pictures, clippings, and other loose material on the designated topic. Before completing your research in the library you should ask the librarian where your library's subject file drawers are and if there is any information available on your topic.

NAME _____

USING THE BIOGRAPHICAL DICTIONARY

Washington, George. 1731–1799. First president of the United States, born Westmorland County, VA, eldest son of Augustine Washington (death 1743), a Virginia planter, and his second wife, Mary Ball (1708–89). Privately educated. County surveyor, Culpeper County, VA (1749). Inherited Mount Vernon after death of Lawrence (1752). Served on General Braddock's staff (1755). Married Martha Curtis (Jan. 6, 1759), widow of Daniel Parke Curtis; retired to Mount Vernon to live life of Virginia gentleman-farmer. Member of First and Second Continental Congress (1774–75). Elected to command all Continental armies (June 15, 1775); won the battle of Princeton; established headquarters at Morristown, NJ (1777). Resigned commission (Dec. 23, 1783) and again retired to Mount Vernon to resume care of plantation.

Called from retirement to preside at federal convention in Philadelphia (1787). Unanimously chosenPresident of the United States under the new constitution; took oath of office in New York City (Apr. 30, 1789). Retired from political life (March 3, 1797). On threat of war with France (1798) accepted commission until his death (Dec. 14, 1799). Buried in tomb on his estate at Mount Vernon. Elected to American Hall of Fame (1900).

Read the entry for Washington. Answer the research questions.

1. Why did Washington not serve a third term as president? _____

2. When was Washington elected to the American Hall of Fame? _____

3. Where did he take the oath of office?   _____

4. What did Washington do after his first retirement? _____

5. Did he win the battle of Princeton?   _____

6. Where was Washington born?   _____

7. In what county was Washington a surveyor?   _____

8. When was he a member of the First and Second Continental Congress?

   _____

9. Was he ever commander in chief of the Virginia troops? _____

10. Where did he establish his headquarters in 1777? _____

PRELIMINARY RESEARCH

What does "preliminary" mean? According to the dictionary preliminary means "preparing for the main action." In your case the "main action" is researching your topic! So before you actually start doing your research and taking notes, you need to do some *preliminary* research.

This phase of your research project is probably the most fun. Now is the time you investigate what sources you are going to use. If your teacher would like you to use one encyclopedia, two books, two magazines, plus one additional source (almanac, atlas, biographical dictionary, vertical file, etc.) you need to look at *more* than just one encyclopedia, more than two books, more than two magazines, etc. You want to find the information that will be the most informative on your topic. How do you do this? Read on.

Your library will likely have more than one set of encyclopedias. Check two or three (or more) and compare the entries on your topic. It would take a long time to read all of the entries, but if you read the first and last paragraphs and the first sentence of some of the subsections in the entry, you will get a good idea of which encyclopedia will be most helpful to you.

When your are looking for your book sources—depending on your topic you may find many books to choose from—check the table of contents and the index for your topic name. Again, decide which books have the most information on your topic and which will be *most helpful* to you when writing your report.

As you are doing your preliminary research keep track of the name of the encyclopedia set you want to use and the call numbers of the books you found most helpful.

Go to the *Reader's Guide* and copy down all the articles that sound relevant to your topic—there may be three or there may be ten. No matter how many, you should look up all of the magazines that have information on your topic. After reading the first and last paragraphs and the first sentences of several paragraphs, decide if the article will help you. If you think you might use a particular magazine issue, check "yes" by the magazine information you wrote down. If you won't be using the article, check "no." (Note: It is ok if you have more than two "yes" checks—remember, this is only preliminary research and you may decide not to use some of your "yes" checks when you actually start your note-taking later.)

CAUTIONARY NOTES ON PRELIMINARY RESEARCH

While you are doing your preliminary research you need to be aware of the dates of the sources you are investigating. You should generally try to use books and magazines that are not more than five years old. With some topics, such as animals, you do not need to be as careful. A book published in 1980 on the polar bear will probably have just as valid information as a book published in 1990.

However, if you are researching any scientific area (space-related, disease-related, etc.) geographic area, or current events topic where new findings are made every year (or month!), it is best that your sources be as current as possible. In fact, magazines and the latest almanac would very likely be your best sources.

As an example situation, you might find an older book that refers to the *forty-eight* states. At one time the U.S. only had forty-eight states—but if you included this information in your report *now*, by accident, you would make your readers suspect about the rest of your report. They would wonder if anything else you've written is untrue.

You should also be aware that you may find conflicting facts in the sources you use. Dates of events especially, may be different depending on the source you use. Do not be overly worried about this. If you can, compare more than two sources to see if a third can help you clarify a fact. Your teacher knows that your information can only be as true as what you find in your research—if you use a date from one source that is listed differently somewhere else, it is ok for you to include either date in your report.

NAME _____

PRELIMINARY RESEARCH CHECKLIST

Before you finish your preliminary research use the checklist below to make sure that you have explored all sources that may be helpful to you. When you have completed the checklist, let the *real* research begin!

☐ I have looked under my topic name in at least two encyclopedias.

☐ I have looked at the books containing information on my topic name in the library.

☐ I have used the Reader's Guide for looking up magazine articles.

☐ I have asked the librarian if he/she knows of any other helpful sources for my report.

Yes   *No*

☐   ☐   Will the almanac be helpful?

☐   ☐   Will the atlas be helpful?

☐   ☐   Will the biographical dictionary be helpful?

☐   ☐   Will the vertical file be helpful?

CHARTS, TIME LINES AND TABLES

While you are reading for information on your topic you will likely come to some charts, (graphs), and time lines. These should not be passed over as unimportant information. If you take the time to study them, these visuals will show you in a vivid, graphic style how facts and ideas relate to one another and how conclusions can be drawn from what you have learned in your reading.

FINDING INFORMATION FROM CHARTS

In order to understand a chart you have to be able to read one correctly. Look at the items below.

Four Basic Steps: Summary Charts

1. Find the basic idea or information that the chart is presenting. You can get this information quickly by checking the title.

2. Break down the large topic into smaller parts of information. You can get this information by quickly checking the titles of each column.

3. Read carefully the details or smaller parts of information in the columns. You can get this information by starting at the top and working through the chart.

4. Understand the information you have studied on the chart. Draw conclusions based on the information that the chart is presenting.

(Note: Make sure you have carefully done the reading on the page where the chart is found – this will help you better understand what the chart is telling you.)

NAME _____

INFORMATION FROM SUMMARY CHARTS
SOME ENDANGERED SPECIES OF ANIMALS

Common name animals	Scientific name	Distribution	Survival problem
American crocodile	*Crocodylus*	Florida, Mexico, Central and South America, Caribbean islands	Overhunted for its hide; habitat destruction
Asiatic lion	*Panthera leo persica*	India	Habitat destruction; overhunted for sport
Black-footed ferret	*Mustela nigripes*	Known only in captivity	Poisoning of prairie dogs, its chief prey
Black rhinoceros	*Diceros biocornis*	South of Sahara in Africa	Habitat destruction; overhunted for its horn
Blue whale	*Balaenoptera musculus*	All oceans	Overhunted for its blubber; for food and for whale oil
Brown pelican	*Pelecanus occidentalis*	North Carolina to Texas, California, West Indies, coastal Central and South America	Contamination of food supply with pesticides
California condor	*Gymnogyps californianus*	Known only in captivity	Habitat destruction; hunted for sport; overcollection of eggs for food
Devils Hole pupfish	*Cyprinodon diabolis*	Nevada	Habitat destruction
Imperial parrot	*Amazona imperialis*	West Indies, Dominica	Habitat destruction; illegal capture for pets

Read the chart. Answer the questions.

1. What are the four sections of information presented in this chart? _____

_____

_____

2. What is the scientific name for the blue whale? _____

3. What are the survival problems of the black rhinoceros? _____

_____

4. Where does the Asiatic lion live? _____

5. What is the range of the American crocodile? _____

_____

6. *Mustela nigripes* is the scientific name for what animal? _____

7. What two animals are known in captivity only? _____

_____

8. What animal has been captured for pets? _____

NAME _____

INFORMATION FROM SUMMARY CHARTS
IMPORTANT SPACE PROBES

Date Launched	Name	Launched by	Accomplishments
1959 Sept. 12	Luna	U.S.S.R.	First probe to strike the moon.
1962 Apr. 23	Ranger 4	U.S.A.	First probe to strike the moon; failed to televise pictures to the earth.
1964 Nov. 28	Mariner 4	U.S.A.	Photographed Mars on July 14, 1965; measured conditions in space.
1966 Jan. 31	Luna 9	U.S.S.R.	Made first soft landing on the moon on Feb. 3; sent 27 pictures to the earth.
Mar. 31	Luna 10	U.S.S.R.	First spacecraft to orbit the moon; began orbiting on April 3.
1967 June 12	Venera 4	U.S.S.R.	First spacecraft to transmit data on Venus' atmosphere.
1968 Sept. 14	Zond 5	U.S.S.R.	First probe to orbit the moon and return to a soft landing on the earth.
1970 Aug. 17	Venera 7	U.S.S.R.	First spacecraft to transmit data from Venus' surface; landed Dec. 15, 1970.
Sept. 12	Luna 16	U.S.S.R.	First unmanned spacecraft to return lunar samples; landed on Sept. 20.
1971 May 28	Mars 3	U.S.S.R.	Carried capsule that made first soft landing on Mars; landed Dec. 2, 1971.
May 30	Mariner 9	U.S.A.	First probe to orbit Mars; began orbiting on Nov. 13, 1971.
1972 Mar. 2	Pioneer 10	U.S.A.	Flew past Jupiter on Dec. 3, 1973, and sent back scientific data; on June 13, 1983, became the first spacecraft to travel beyond all the planets.

Read the chart. Answer the questions.

1. What are the four sections presented in this chart? _____

_____

2. What spacecraft made the first soft landing on the moon on Feb. 3?

_____

3. What was the first spacecraft to orbit the moon? _____

4. The Luna 16 was launched on what date? _____

5. What country sent the first probe to Mars? _____

6. On April 23, 1962, the U.S.A. sent what spacecraft to the moon? _____

7. What was the first spacecraft to transmit data on Venus' atmosphere?

_____

8. The Pioneer 10 flew past what planet in 1973? _____

FINDING INFORMATION FROM TIME LINES

In order to use information in your report from a time line, you need to know how to read one. There are four basic steps in reading a time line.

Four Basic Steps: Reading a Time line

1. Know what the time line is about. (Read the title or leading time line.)

2. Know the time period of the time line. (Read the first and last dates of the time line.)

3. Know the pattern of the dates listed. (Is there any pattern to the dates? For example: 20 years, 40 years, 60 years, 80 years.) There is a pattern of every 20 years.

4. Know the connection among the items listed on the time line. (If there are all the dates of presidential elections and the candidates for president, know that the timeline talks about American presidents in history.)

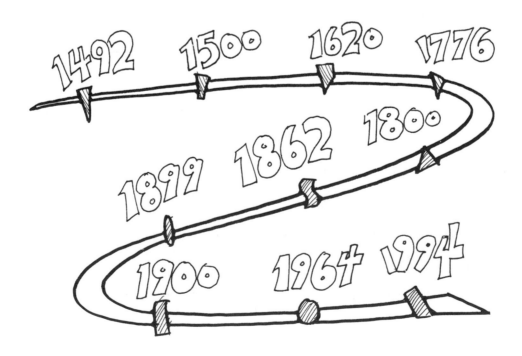

NAME _____

FINDING INFORMATION FROM TIME LINES
MAJOR EVENTS IN AMERICAN HISTORY
1787–1848

1787	The founding fathers wrote the constitution.
1790's	The first U.S. political parties developed.
1790	Samuel Slater built the country's first successful water-powered machines for spinning cotton.
1793	Eli Whitney developed a toothed cotton gin.
1800	Washington D.C. became the national capital.
1803	The Louisiana Purchase almost doubled the size of the United States.
1811	Work began on the national road, which – when completed – linked the east and the midwest.
1812-1815	The United States and Great Britain fought the War of 1812.
1814	Francis Scott Key wrote "The Star Spangled Banner."
1820	The Missouri Compromise ended a slavery dispute.
1823	The Monroe Doctrine warned Europeans against interference in Western Hemisphere affairs.
1825	The Erie Canal opened, providing a water route from the Atlantic Ocean to the Great Lakes.
1830	South Carolina threatened secession over a tariff.
1834	Samuel F.B. Morse demonstrated the first successful telegraph in the United States.
1846	Britain ceded the southern part of the Oregon Country to the United States.
1848	Victory in the Mexican War gave the United States vast new territory in the West.
1848	The discovery of gold in California triggered the Gold Rush.

Read the chart. Answer the questions.

1. What time period does this time line cover in American history? _____

2. What four major events took place between 1820 and 1830? _____

_____

_____

_____

3. How long did the War of 1812 last? _____

4. In what year did Washington D.C. become the national capital? _____

5. In 1837, who demonstrated the first successful telegraph? _____

_____

6. In what year did Francis Scott Key write "The Star Spangled Banner?"

_____

7. What body of water provided a water route from the Atlantic Ocean to the
Great Lakes?_____

NAME _____

FINDING INFORMATION FROM TIME LINES
WORLD WAR I

Read the time line. Answer the questions.

1. What time period does this time line cover in history? _____

2. What month and year was Archduke Ferdinand assassinated? _____

3. What two events took place in March 1918?_____

   _____

4. Who began their final attack in September 1918? _____

5. When did Britain and Austria-Hungary declare war on Germany?

   _____

6. What major event took place in July 1916? _____

   _____

7. When did the United States enter World War I?_____

8. When did Italy enter the war? _____

9. What major event took place in November 1918? _____

   _____

FINDING INFORMATION FROM TIME LINES
EARLY EXPLORERS

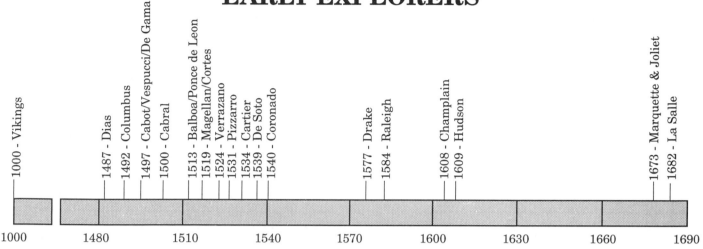

Read the time line. Answer the questions.

1. What time period does this time line cover in history? _____

2. What is the date for Drake? _____

3. What is the date for La Salle? _____

4. Is 1608 the correct date for Champlain? _____

5. Between what two major dates did most of the exploration take place?

   _____

6. In what year are both Balboa and Ponce de Leon given credit for early explorations? _____

7. Name the two explorers in the 1570-1600 time period? _____

   _____

8. Between what two major dates did no major explorations take place?

   _____

9. Name the explorers in the 1660-1690 time period? _____

   _____

MY OWN TIME LINE

Design your own time line about your life. Include birthdays and events that were important to you.

FINDING INFORMATION FROM TABLES

Finding information from tables requires several skills. You, the researcher, need to know how to read this type of research information. There are five basic steps to reading a table for research information.

Five Basic Steps: Reading a Table

1. Know what the table is about. (Read the heading or title of the table for this information.)

2. Know what each section means. (Read the titles of headings of each section.)

3. Know what the measurement units are. (Are the measurements in feet or inches? Are the measurements in minutes or hours? Find out.)

4. Know about any extra information given in the table. (Read any special notes about the table.)

5. Know what conclusions you can draw from the information.

FINDING INFORMATION FROM TABLES
SUPER BOWL

YEAR	WINNER	LOSER	SITE
1967	Green Bay Packers, 35	Kansas City Chiefs, 10	Los Angeles, Coliseum
1968	Green Bay Packers, 33	Oakland Raiders, 14	Orange Bowl, Miami
1969	New York Jets, 16	Baltimore Colts, 7	Orange Bowl, Miami
1970	Kansas City Chiefs, 23	Minnesota Vikings, 7	Tulane Stadium, New Orleans
1971	Baltimore Colts, 16	Dallas Cowboys, 13	Orange Bowl, Miami
1972	Dallas Cowboys, 24	Miami Dolphins, 3	Tulane Stadium, New Orleans
1973	Miami Dolphins, 14	Washington Redskins, 7	Los Angeles Coliseum
1974	Miami Dolphins, 24	Minnesota Vikings, 7	Rice Stadium, Houston
1975	Pittsburgh Steelers, 16	Minnesota Vikings, 6	Tulane Stadium, New Orleans
1976	Pittsburgh Steelers, 21	Dallas Cowboys, 17	Orange Bowl, Miami
1977	Oakland Raiders, 32	Minnesota Vikings, 14	Rose Bowl, Pasadena
1978	Dallas Cowboys, 27	Denver Broncos, 10	Superdome, New Orleans
1979	Pittsburgh Steelers, 35	Dallas Cowboys, 31	Orange Bowl, Miami
1980	Pittsburgh Steelers, 31	Los Angeles Rams, 19	Rose Bowl, Pasadena
1981	Oakland Raiders, 27	Philadelphia Eagles, 10	Superdome, New Orleans
1982	San Francisco 49ers, 26	Cincinatti Bengals, 21	Silverdome, Pontiac, MI
1983	Washington Redskins, 27	Miami Dolphins, 17	Rose Bowl, Pasadena
1984	Los Angeles Raiders, 38	Washington Redskins, 9	Tampa Stadium
1985	San Francisco 49ers, 38	Miami Dolphins, 16	Standford Stadium, Palo Alto, CA
1986	Chicago Bears, 46	New England Patriots, 10	Superdome, New Orleans

Read the time line. Answer the questions.

1. What four sections are presented in the Super Bowl table? _____
   _____

2. Who was the winner in 1975? _____

3. Where was the 1986 game played? _____

4. What was the score for the 1967 game? _____

5. Who played against the New York Jets in 1969? _____

6. The Minnesota Vikings played against the Kansas City Chiefs in what
   years? _____

7. What was the score of the Miami Dolphins in 1985? _____

8. What was the score in 1986 for the Chicago Bears? _____

9. Was 31 the score for the Dallas Cowboys in 1979? _____

10. What was the score for the Washington Redskins in 1983? _____

NAME _____

FINDING INFORMATION FROM TABLES
FASTEST SCHEDULED TRAIN RUNS
IN U.S. AND CANADA

RAILROAD	TRAIN	FROM	TO	DIS. MILES	TIME MIN.	SPEED MPH
Amtrak	Three Metroliners	Baltimore	Wilmington	68.4	42	97.8
Amtrak	Metroliner 101	Metro Park	Prince Junction	23.9	15	95.6
Amtrak	Eight Metroliners	Baltimore	Wilmington	68.4	43	95.4
Amtrak	Three Metroliners	Wilmington	Baltimore	68.4	45	91.2
Amtrak	Eight Metroliners	Wilmington	Baltimore	68.4	46	89.2
Amtrak	Four trains	Rensseleleur	Hudson	28.0	19	88.4
Amtrak	Three Metroliners	Newark	Philadelphia	80.5	56	86.2
Amtrak	Three trains	Baltimore	Wilmington	68.4	48	85.5
Amtrak	Garden State Special	Aberdeen	Wilmington	38.3	27	85.1
Amtrak	Two Metroliners	Metro Park	Philadelphia	66.4	47	84.8
Amtrak	Virginian	Trenton	Metro Park	33.9	34	84.7
Amtrak	Five Metroliners	Newark	Philadelphia	80.5	57	84.7
Amtrak	Three trains	Baltimore	Wilmington	68.4	48	83.8
Amtrak	Three Metroliners	Philadelphia	Newark	80.5	58	83.3
Amtrak	Independence	Newark(Del)	Baltimore	56.8	47	83.1
Via Rail Canada	Five trains	Guildwood	Kingston	145.1	105	82.9

Read the time line. Answer the questions.

1. What seven sections are listed in this table? _____

_____

_____

2. How is the distance measured in this table? _____ _____

3. What are the two railroads listed? _____

4. How is time measured in this table? _____

5. What is the time listed for the Independence train? _____

6. Where does the Virginian leave from? _____

7. What is the speed (mph) of the Garden State Special? _____

8. The Three Metroliners leave Baltimore and arrive where? _____

9. What is the speed (mph) of the Metroliner 101? _____

10. Where does the Garden State Special leave from? _____

SKIMMING

Skimming is a technique you can use in your preliminary research as you are deciding which sources you want to use for your report.

When you skim you read quickly through an article or chapter and try to understand the main idea and key points without slowing down for details. Skimming is an especially helpful reading technique when you are exploring a lengthy article or chapter on your topic.

By skimming – reading much faster than you would at normal speed – you can get an overall feel for what is important in the material quickly so that you can move on to investigation of your next source.

Skim paragraph 1 below. Then record five important points (on the next page) that you remember from skimming the paragraph. Then skim paragraph 2 and record five key points that you remember from this paragraph.

PARAGRAPH 1

How do you bake cookies? First, put all the ingredients out on the table. This makes it easy to begin. Second, read the recipe carefully. Do you have all the ingredients that you will need? Now set the oven at the temperature the recipe calls for. It is important to have the oven hot for the cookies to bake well. Next mix the ingredients as the recipe tells you. Shape the cookies and put them on a flat cookie sheet. Bake. Then cool the cookies. And that's how you bake cookies.

PARAGRAPH 2

How do you choose a book for your report? First, learn exactly what the assignment will be. If you do this, it will help you to know what to look for. Next, ask yourself how long must the book be? Often, your teachers will give you an idea of how many pages you must read. And, ask yourself what type book do I need to choose? Do you need a mystery book? A biography? Or a science fiction book? Now you can check the shelves. When you find a book that interests you, do three things. Read the dust jacket. This will give you an idea of the book's contents. Skim the table of contents. This will give you more information about the book. Check the author. Is it an author whose other books you have read and liked? Now check your book out!

NAME _____

SKIMMING

Skim the paragraphs on page 68. Write five details for each paragraph.

PARAGRAPH 1

1. _____

_____

2. _____

_____

3. _____

_____

4. _____

_____

5. _____

_____

PARAGRAPH 2

1. _____

_____

2. _____

_____

3. _____

_____

4. _____

_____

5. _____

_____

FREEWRITING

After you have completed your preliminary research and have looked up information on your topic in several sources, now you are free to freewrite.

In many ways freewriting is like brainstorming. When you freewrite you write about everything you can remember reading about your topic during your preliminary research. Unlike brainstorming, however, you have your topic and now you need to come up with ideas of what you want to discuss about your topic in your paper. Write down whatever comes to mind: phrases, comparisons, thoughts, and questions especially – anything having to do with your topic. Again, like brainstorming, do not worry about spelling, grammar, or penmanship.

Perhaps the most important part of the freewriting process is question-writing. Questions that you hope to answer in your paper. By having these questions written out before you, it will be easier later on to place the information you find in your source under the corresponding questions you asked yourself while freewriting.

Look at the following example of freewriting below:

Topic: Falcons

What do falcons eat? Where do they live? How many kinds are there? How long do they live? Is anything being done to protect them? How are they different from hawks? Define raptor. Do different kinds of falcons have different coloring? Falcons as pets, falconing. Medieval history of falcons. Do falcons have any enemies? What is the purpose of the hood that is sometimes seen on falconer's falcons?

FREEWRITING QUESTIONS

RESEARCH TOPIC: _____

Questions my research report should answer:

1. _____

2. _____

3. _____

4. _____

5. _____

6. _____

7. _____

8. _____

9. _____

10. _____

11. _____

12. _____

13. _____

14. _____

15. _____

16. _____

17. _____

18. _____

19. _____

20. _____

TAKING NOTES

After you have finished your preliminary research and have explored all of the possible sources of information for your report, you can begin taking notes from the sources you have decided to use.

Do you remember the questions you wrote down when you did freewriting on your topic? Get these questions out of your research folder and have them in front of you as you begin taking notes. When you come to a fact or information that answers or relates to one of the questions – this is what you should take notes on.

For taking notes you will use the larger-sized index cards (4 x 6) to write on. On one card you should have notes from only one source and pertaining to only one specific area of your topic. Color-coding your cards is a good idea. Have five different colored markers (or a color for each of your sources) and mark an "x" on all the cards from one source in one color and a different colored "x" on all the cards from a different source. (For example: Put a blue "x" on all the cards that you have from the *World Book Encyclopedia,* a red "x" on your cards from *Newsweek* magazine and a green "x" for your cards from the biographical dictionary you are using.) Although the color-coding may seem confusing at first, it will help you remember which sources your notes came from.

As you take notes from each source, you will use the smaller note cards (3 x 5) to make out bibliography cards to use in your bibliography at the end of your report. On page 107 you will find a sample bibliography page. Using the information you see for each type of source (encyclopedia, book, magazine, etc.) copy down this exact information on your small index cards for each source you take notes from. If you are using a book, include the call number on the cards as well. (Note: when copying down the bibliography information from each source, use the marker color that corresponds to your large note cards.)

At the end of your paper, on the bibliography page, you will list all of the sources that you took notes on in your research. This list needs to be in alphabetical order by author name. Since you made each source its own (small) note card it will be easy for you to arrange the cards in the correct author order. This way you will not get confused when writing your bibliography page.

3 X 5 REPRODUCIBLE NOTE TAKING CARDS

Source: _____

Subheading/Topic: _____

_____

_____

_____

_____

_____

Source: _____

Subheading/Topic: _____

_____

_____

_____

_____

_____

4 X 6 REPRODUCIBLE NOTE TAKING CARDS

Source: _____

Topic: _____

Question/Subheading: _____

_____

_____

_____

_____

_____

_____

Source: _____

Topic: _____

Question/Subheading: _____

_____

_____

_____

_____

_____

_____

BIBLIOGRAPHY NOTE TAKING CARDS

BOOK BIBLIOGRAPHY CARD

Author: _____

Title: _____

Place of Publication: _____

Publisher: _____

Copyright Date: _____ Pages: _____

ENCYCLOPEDIA BIBLIOGRAPHY CARD

Author:(if given) _____

Title of Article: _____

Name of Encyclopedia: _____

Copyright Date: _____ Volume: _____

Pages: _____

MAGAZINE BIBLIOGRAPHY CARD

Author:(if given) _____

Title of Article: _____

Name of Magazine: _____

Volume Number: _____ Date: _____

Pages: _____

NOTE-TAKING TIPS

When you first start taking notes in a research situation, you may have a difficult time writing them down correctly. The following tips should help you:

1. Read the entire article or chapter before you start taking any notes – it's best to get an overview of what you are reading first to make sure you only take notes on what you need.

2. Go back over the material and carefully select the information you want to include in your report. Stick with your chosen topic. Unless something seems very important, try to take notes only on information that answers the questions you wrote down during your freewriting.

3. Label each note card at the top with the subheading or the questions that it answers.

4. When you come to a fact or an idea that you think will be helpful in your report, close the book or magazine you are reading, think about what you have read, and then write down the fact or information in your own words. By closing the book before you take your notes, you ensure that you've understood what you've read; this also is a safeguard against copying straight out of the book. Copying the exact words out of a book is called plagiarism . You must use your own words.

5. Facts, measurements, dates, or other statistics are okay to copy. This information belongs to everyone. Make sure that you use these facts in sentences with your own words.

6. If you find a paragraph that you want to take notes on, it's best to sum up the paragraph in just two or three sentences in a way that the paragraph makes sense to you. Shortening a full paragraph into a few sentences in your own words is called paraphrasing.

7. If you want to use the author's words (you may want to do this if the author is expressing an opinion), copy the part down exactly and write down the page number where the quote is found. When you exactly write the quote in your report you will put these "borrowed words" in quotation marks.

ORGANIZING AN OUTLINE

After you have taken all of your notes, you can begin organizing your outline. Why do you need an outline? An outline will give you a clear understanding of how your report will be structured. It will also help you decide exactly what you want to say. An outline will help keep you from going off on tangents when you actually start writing your report. You can refer to your outline to remember exactly what you are writing about, and in what order your information should be in.

When making an outline, think of it as a map – a map that is guiding you from the beginning of your report to the end. What does your reader need to know first? Pretend you are explaining your topic to a friend. What would you explain first? Second? Third? – So that the order would be logical and your friend could understand you?

The outline, like your report, should have a beginning, middle, and end. Your beginning is the *introduction;* here you explain what you will be talking about in your report. You are letting the reader know what is ahead. The middle part is called the *body* of your report; here is where you give the reader all the details. The end is called the *conclusion;* here is where you "wrap-up" your report.

To make your report easier to write, try to group your note cards into three sections. All the cards in each respective section should relate to the same general subtopic.

When you organize the middle part, or the body of your report, decide if your report follows a chronological pattern. If you are doing your report on a person, the chronological order of your cards will probably work best. Arrange the cards by the order in which the facts occurred in time.

If your report is more scientific in nature, ordering your cards from the general to specific might work best, that is, start with the main body of your report writing about a general aspect of your topic. In the next section get more specific, and in the section right before the conclusion you will be the most specific.

Perhaps your notes break down nicely into three distinct subtopic groups that are equally specific. If this is the case you may not need a particular order – just make sure the cards are in their three distinct sections. Look at the outline diagrams on page 79. Refer to these diagrams as you plan your own outline. Because you've taken notes on note cards it should be easy to lay out the cards and experiment rearranging them until you find a workable outline. (Do not write out all of the information on the cards at this point – only the main idea of each card.)

OUTLINE TIPS

1. Include only the key points in your outline. Do not list any of the supporting details until you actually write your report.

2. You may want to do more than one outline before you write your report. The first "rough" outline would be the most basic with only one or two-word phrases labeling each section. A second outline will be more specific and have more facts filled in. Your third outline might be very close to what your actual report would look like. Remember: The better and more detailed your outline, the easier it will be to write your report.

3. No matter how detailed your outline, always leave the specific supporting details out – they will clutter the outline.

4. You probably took more notes than you will include in your outline. Be selective in your writing – you do not need to include everything you took notes on.

5. In your conclusion you will either:
   - A) Sum up, or repeat the main idea.
   - B) Give your personal opinion on the topic, or
   - C) Give a "predictive" closing. (You would likely use this type of conclusion with a current-event related topic.)

   You might start your conclusion with words like, "therefore," "finally," "in conclusion," etc.

6. Take a close look at the outlines on the following page!

OUTLINE DIAGRAMS

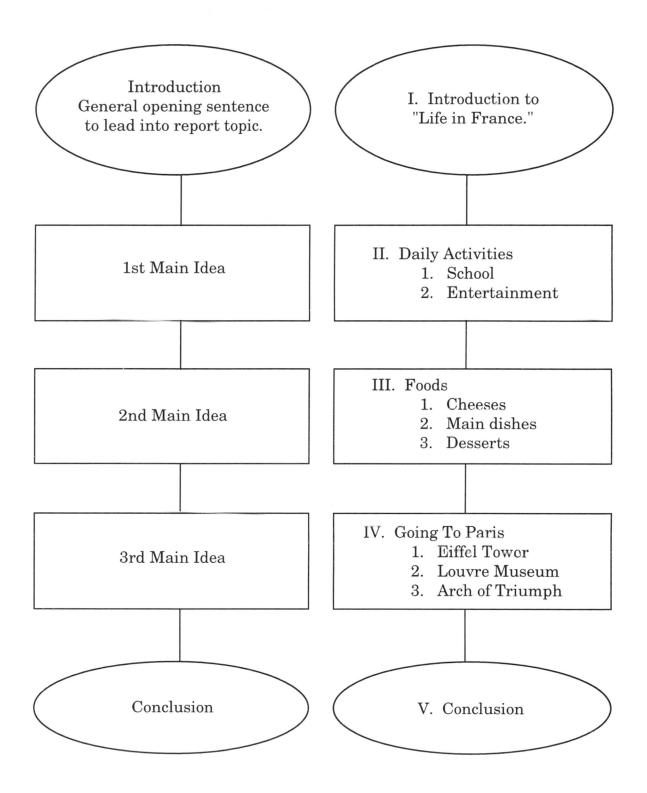

Introduction
General opening sentence
to lead into report topic.

I. Introduction to
"Life in France."

1st Main Idea

II. Daily Activities
    1. School
    2. Entertainment

2nd Main Idea

III. Foods
    1. Cheeses
    2. Main dishes
    3. Desserts

3rd Main Idea

IV. Going To Paris
    1. Eiffel Tower
    2. Louvre Museum
    3. Arch of Triumph

Conclusion

V. Conclusion

EVALUATING YOUR RESEARCH: IS IT FACT OR OPINION?

When you collect research *facts*, you should know if you have collected facts or *opinions*. A fact is a statement that is accurate. It has truth. It can be checked as being true. An opinion is a belief. It is what someone thinks or believes. It may or may not be true.

A fact can be supported by other facts. There are certain words that may signal to you that you have collected an opinion. Words such as *believe*, *feel*, *think*, *better*, or *even more* may be a signal that you have an opinion not a fact.

Let's say that you collect two research statements. The first: scientists believe more money should be spent in studying space. The second: scientist have been studying problems in space. Which is fact? Which is opinion? The first is an opinion. Notice the word "believe" and "more" are used. The second statement is a fact. It can be supported by other facts.

NAME _____

IS IT FACT OR OPINION?

Read each statement. Your research may be fact or opinion. If the statement is fact write "fact." If the statement is opinion, write "opinion."

Example:

1. There are better ways to write your report. _____ *opinion*_____

2. You need to know what is fact and what is opinion when writing a research report. _____ *fact*_____

1. There are many scientists studying the universe._____

2. We need more scientists than we need other workers._____

3. We are studying our environment to learn better ways of living.

   _____

4. I feel animals are an important part of our environment.

   _____

5. I feel it is healthier to eat vegetables. _____

6. Nutritionists believe that we do not know enough about vitamins.

   _____

7. The more vitamins you take, the better your health will be.

   _____

8. Scientists are studying the effects of vitamins. _____

9. I believe the space program is good. _____

10. Scientists are studying the space program. _____

11. History can always be studied. _____

12. It is better to study early history than recent history._____

13. You should always study something new. _____

14. Learning is growing. _____

15. There are 250 million people in the U.S. _____

NAME _____

IS IT FACT OR OPINION?

Read each statement. Your research may be fact or opinion. If the statement is fact write "fact." If the statement is opinion, write "opinion."

1. I think students should study what they like to learn. _____

2. Schools present many subjects for students to study. _____

3. Television is better for young people than other types of entertainment.

   _____

4. Television offers many different kinds of programs. _____

5. I believe homework helps make students smarter. _____

6. I think we need to learn better ways of eating. _____

7. Scientists say too many fats in the diet are unhealthy. _____

8. Brown eggs are not better than white eggs. _____

9. I believe white eggs are better. _____

10. The space program supports many people. _____

11. The space program is better than it was before. _____

12. We have many scientists in the U.S. _____

13. Studying helps improve your learning. _____

14. Homework helps you learn. _____

15. There are many automobiles in the U.S. _____

SUPPORTING YOUR RESEARCH STATEMENTS

When you organize your research statements, you will need to know what type of information you have collected. There are five basic types of statements.

- You may collect a **fact**. A fact is a statement that can be checked for its truth. For example: *The floppy disk was invented by IBM in 1970.*

- You can collect an **example**. An example gives types or kinds of a given thing. For example: *There are four different types of kites. They are the delta, the box, the flat, and the bow.*

- You can collect a **story**. You can use a story or a personal experience. For example: *Let me tell you about our vacation.*

- You can collect a **definition**. A definition explains something. For example: *A motet, is a musical composition usually sung without instrumentation.*

- And last, you can collect a **quote**. A quote is the words of someone written exactly as they were said. For example: *"Important principles may and must be inflexible." (Abraham Lincoln).*

NAME _____

SUPPORTING YOUR RESEARCH STATEMENTS

Read the research statements below. Is it an example? (1) A quotation? (2) A fact or statistic? (3) A story (personal experience)? (4) Or a definition? (5). Write example, quotation, fact, story, or definition for each statement.

1. _____ There are one million kites sold in the U.S. yearly.

2. _____ Kites are known to have been built in early China.

3. _____ Let me tell you how I found my dog.

4. _____ A kite is an object that flies in the sky. It is made with paper and string. And always has a tail.

5. _____ Many types of kites exist. There are five basic types of kites: the box kite, flat kite, bowed kite, delta kite, and the flexible kite.

6. _____ The flat kite is a kite that always has a tail that is seven times its length.

7. _____ Safety rules for flying kites include; (1) fly in the open, (2) never fly in bad weather, (3) be certain your kite is well made.

8. _____ Let me tell you about the biggest kite I ever flew.

9. _____ There are over 10,000 kites flown yearly in the U.S.

10. _____ "Eureka!" said Benjamin Franklin after he flew his kite.

NAME _____

SUPPORTING YOUR RESEARCH STATEMENTS

Read the research statements below. Is it an example? (1) A quotation? (2) A fact or statistic? (3) A story (personal experience)? (4) Or a definition? (5). Write example, quotation, fact, story, or definition for each statement.

1. _____ Ben Franklin said: "A penny saved is a penny earned!"

2. _____ Let me tell you about the funniest day I ever had.

3. _____ Safety rules for swimming include: (1) do not swim alone, (2) do not swim in unsafe waters, (3) do not swim after eating a heavy meal.

4. _____ There are over one million dolls sold in the U.S. yearly.

5. _____ "Can you hear me?" asked Alexander Bell.

6. _____ There are over 1,000 types of ants.

7. _____ Reptiles can be found in the mountains.

8. _____ Let me tell you about my camping trip.

10. _____ Let me tell you how to save money when shopping.

NAME _____

SUPPORTING YOUR RESEARCH STATEMENTS
OVERVIEW

Read the research statements below. Is it an example? (1) A quotation? (2) A fact or statistic? (3) A story (personal experience)? (4) Or a definition? (5). Write example, quotation, fact, story, or definition for each statement.

1. _____ Let me tell you about my good grades.

2. _____ An ant has three major body parts.

3. _____ "Don't give up the ship!" yelled the captain.

4. _____ "Don't tread on me!" said the colonists.

5. _____ There are over 250 million people in the United

States.

6. _____ Let me tell you the strangest thing that ever

happened to me.

7. _____ There are two official languages in Canada.

8. _____ There are 10 points on the Richter Earthquake

Scale.

9. _____ Let me tell you how I first learned to cook.

10. _____ Running can damage your knees.

WRITING YOUR REPORT

If you have made a good outline, writing your report should go smoothly.

Before you start writing, lay your outline near you and arrange all of your note cards (the ones you've decided to use) in the order that you had them when you wrote your outline. When you have your note cards arranged according to their subtopic headings, you are ready to start writing your report. If your outline is very detailed and complete, you may essentially just be writing your outline with connecting sentences and the supportive details that you did not include previously.

While you are writing the report, for variety, try to use both long and short sentences. Be creative with your sentence-making – don't always start the same way. For example: if you're writing about the kangaroo, don't always start sentences "The kangaroo..."

When you come to a note card that has quoted material that you want to include in the report, use the following format directly after the quoted passage "(author last name, page #)." So if you were using a quote from page 58 of a book by C.S. Lewis, you would follow the quote with : (Lewis 58). You do not need a comma between the last name and the page number.

When you finish your report, don't forget to include the bibliography page of sources you used in your paper. Refer to the example format on page 107 if you need help.

Before you turn in your report, you need to proof it to make sure it has no mistakes that you have overlooked. The proofing checklist on page 108 will help you remember which types of mistakes to look out for when you proofread your report.

NAME _____

CHECKLIST FOR REPORT WRITING

Before you start writing your final report you should know exactly what is expected of you. If your teacher has not told you already, be sure to find out the following:

Do I need a cover for my report?   YES   NO

Do I need visuals, such as maps, time lines, or pictures?   YES   NO

Should I number the pages?   YES   NO

How long should the report be? _____ pages.

Should I use pencil, pen, or have it typed? (circle one)

Should I double space (skip a line) or use every line? (circle one)

Should I use just one side of my paper or both sides? (circle one)

Where should my name go? _____

DATE DUE:_____

WRITING THE FOOTNOTE—
THE BOOK

Writing footnotes is simple. Always write the author's name first, then write the name of the book and the page on which you found the information. When do you write a footnote? And what is a footnote?

You footnote when you find a piece of information that you are using in your report. This includes when you "take" information *word for word* from a research source. If you do this, put quotation marks around those words. A footnote tells you where you have been in the magazine, book, or encyclopedia. It specifically notes what information you have taken. We call this notation *citing your references*. It is called a *citation*.

Let's say you found a fact about boats in a book called, *Story of Boats* written by T.H. Sail. How would you write the footnote?

Write: T.H. Sail, <u>The Story of Boats</u>, p 10.

WRITING THE FOOTNOTE—THE BOOK

Read the information below. Rewrite it in correct footnote form.

1. You found your fact on page 13 of, *How to Cook* written by Peter Baker.

   _____

2. You found your fact on page 58 of, *The Key* written by Peter Stick.

   _____

3. You found your fact on page 17 of, *Science Experiments* written by J. Space.

   _____

4. You found your fact on page 42 of, *History of the Comics* written by R. Cartoon.

   _____

5. You found your fact on page 9 of, *Planets* written by Peter Ring.

   _____

6. You found your fact on page 7 of, *Flowers* written by J. Bloom.

   _____

7. You found your fact on page 13 of, *Racing* by C. Speck.

   _____

WRITING THE FOOTNOTE—THE BOOK

Read the information below. Rewrite it in correct footnote form.

1. You found your fact on page 47 of, *Whales* written by T. Sea.

   _____

2. You found your fact on page 27 of, *Science* written by J. Weather.

   _____

3. You found your fact on page 39 of, *Wild Animals* written by Peter Long.

   _____

4. You found your fact on page 51 of, *Nutrition* written by J. Vitamin.

   _____

5. You found your fact on page 88 of, *Vitamins* by R. Carrot.

   _____

6. You found your fact on page 8 of, *Training Your Dog* written by J. Collar.

   _____

7. You found your fact on page 19 of, *History of the United States* written by Peter World.

   _____

WRITING THE FOOTNOTE—
THE MAGAZINE

When you write a footnote for a magazine, always keep in mind that the title of the magazine is included. This makes it easier for anyone reading your footnotes to find the magazine article. The author's name is written first. Then write the title of the article in quotes. Underline the name of the magazine. The underlining makes it easy to see that it is the name of the magazine. And always include the date of the magazine. This will make it easier to find the magazine. And last, write the page number of the first page of the magazine article.

Let's say that you found an article called "How to Fly a Kite" in Hobby Digest (April 17, 1986) on page 17. The article was written by John Rogers.

Write: Rogers, John. "How to Fly a Kite", <u>Hobby Digest</u>, April 17, 1986, 17.

NAME _____

WRITING THE FOOTNOTE—THE MAGAZINE

Read the following information. Then write it in footnote form.

1. You found your fact on page 13 of "Reptiles: Their Stories" in *Science Digest* (April 17, 1989). It was written by Peter Tail.

    _____

2. You found your fact on page 4 of "Snakes" in *Science Digest* (May 13, 1987). It was written by James Slink.

    _____

3. You found your fact on page 9 of "Birds" in *Bird* Magazine (June 17, 1989). It was written by Roger Feather.

    _____

4. You found your fact on page 21 of "Stars" in *Science World* (Oct. 11, 1989). It was written by James Space.

    _____

5. You found your fact on page 37 of "Dogs" in *Animal World* (April 7, 1987) It was written by T. Bowser.

    _____

6. You found your fact on page 12 in "How to Train Your Puppy" in *Dog Digest* (April 19, 1992) by Peter Collar.

    _____

7. You found your fact on page 36 in "Weather and You" in *Science Times* (April 20, 1987) by James Forecast.

    _____

WRITING THE FOOTNOTE—THE MAGAZINE

Read the following information. Then write it in footnote form.

1. You found your fact on page 81 of "Cats" in *Animal World* (June 12, 1989). It was written by T. Purr.

   _____

2. You found your fact on page 33 of "Boats" in *Sports World* (Nov. 11, 1989). It was written by C. Wave.

   _____

3. You found your fact on page 34 of "History of the Teddy Bear" in *Toy World* (July 5, 1987). It was written by T. Bear.

   _____

4. You found your fact on page 17 of "Nutrition and You" in *Health Magazine* (May 16, 1989). It was written by J. Vitamin.

   _____

5. You found your fact on page 53 of "How to Write a Story" in *Story Magazine* (July 10, 1989). It was written by Peter Page.

   _____

6. You found your fact on page 38 in "Skateboarding Across America" in *Hobby Digest* (Sept. 8, 1989) by J.T. Board.

   _____

7. You found your fact on page 65 of "Hairstyles of Today" in *Fashion Magazine* (Aug. 26, 1989) by Barbara Spray.

   _____

WRITING THE FOOTNOTE— ENCYCLOPEDIA

Writing the footnote for an encyclopedia is simple. First, write the name of the encyclopedia article you are using. Write the name in quotes. A comma follows the name. Next, write the title of the encyclopedia. The title is underlined. A comma follows, then the year that the encyclopedia was published. The year is also called the edition. It is important to write the edition of the encyclopedia that you are using. Remember, an article about a particular topic, may be in the 1986 edition, but not in the 1989 edition.

Let's say that you found your information about Paul Revere in an article called "Paul Revere" in the Encyclopedia of History. The edition is 1986.

Write: "Paul Revere," <u>Encyclopedia of History</u>, 1986.

WRITING THE FOOTNOTE— ENCYCLOPEDIA

Read the information below. Rewrite in footnote form.

1. Your information is on page 13 of *Encyclopedia of Science* (1989) in an article called "Insects."

   _____

2. Your information is on page 39 of *Encyclopedia of Animals* (1987) in an article called "Birds of the World."

   _____

3. Your information is on page 57 of *Encyclopedia of Transportation* (1987) in an article called "Sports and Safety Rules."

   _____

4. Your information is on page 7 of *Encyclopedia of Wild Animals* in an article called "Penguins."

   _____

5. Your information is on page 70 of *Encyclopedia of Animals* (1989) in an article called "Zebras."

   _____

6. Your fact is in the 1987 *Encyclopedia of History* in an article called "History of the Zebra."

   _____

7. Your fact is in the 1989 *Encyclopedia of Transportation* in an article called "Boats and Races."

   _____

8. Your fact is in the 1989 *Encyclopedia of Science* in an article called "Sandstorms and Weather."

   _____

9. Your fact is in the 1987 *Encyclopedia of Cooking* in an article called "Japanese Cooking."

   _____

10. Your fact is in the 1986 *Encyclopedia of Games* in an article called "Learning Chess."

    _____

WRITING THE FOOTNOTE—
ENCYCLOPEDIA

Read the information below. Rewrite in footnote form.

1. Your fact is in the 1989 *Encyclopedia of Clothing* in the article "The History of the Shoe."

   _____

2. Your fact is in the 1987 *Encyclopedia of Dogs* in an article called "Training Your Puppy."

   _____

3. Your fact is in the 1989 *Encyclopedia of Wild Animals* in an article called "Lions and Bears."

   _____

4. Your fact is in the 1987 edition of *Encyclopedia of Hobbies* in an article called "Making Kites."

   _____

5. Your fact is in the 1989 edition of *Encyclopedia of Hobbies* in an article called "Collecting Coins."

   _____

6. Your fact is on page 13 of *Encyclopedia of Transportation* (1987) in an article called "Cars of Tomorrow" by John Motor.

   _____

7. Your fact is on page 3 of the 1987 *Encyclopedia of Health* in an article by Peter Smile called "Sports and Health."

   _____

8. Your fact is on page 32 of the 1989 *Encyclopedia of Toys* in an article called "History of the Doll."

   _____

9. Your fact is on page 63 of the 1987 *Encyclopedia of Flowers* in an article called "Starting Your Garden."

   _____

10. Your fact is on page 10 of the 1989 *Encyclopedia of Sports* in an article called "Sports Legends."

   _____

WRITING THE BIBLIOGRAPHY— THE BOOK

Now that you have written your report you must tell what resources you have used. If you used books, magazines, or encyclopedias to write your report, you need to say so by including a ***bibliography*** in your report. A bibliography is an alphabetized list of resources. It is alphabetized by the writers' last names. The form is somewhat different for a book, an encyclopedia, and a magazine.

You can learn a lot from reading a bibliography. Rather than "read" the shelves or card catalog, read a bibliography in the back of a book! You can get a good idea of what resources you can collect for your report. And in the same way, someone reading your bibliography can learn about the sources you used for your report.

Let's look at a book entry for a bibliography. Let's say you found some of the information for your report on sailboats in *The Story of Boats*. It was written by T.H. Sail in Boatweave, New Jersey, in 1989 by Wave Press Publishers.

Your bibliography will look like this:

Sail, T.H. *The Story of Boats*. Boatweave, New Jersey: Wave Press, 1989.

NAME _____

WRITING A BIBLIOGRAPHY—THE BOOK

Read the information below. Then write it in the correct bibliography form.

1. *Your Aquarium,* was published in Deepsea, New Jersey in 1985. It was written by Peter Fish and published by Scale Press.

   _____

2. *All About Ants,* was published by Hill Press in Anthill, Ohio in 1987. It was written by John Picnic.

   _____

3. *The History of Space,* was published by Star Press in Startown, New Jersey in 1989. It was written by Peter Spacecraft.

   _____

4. *Sports,* by John Game was published in 1987 by Goal Press in Endtown, New York.

   _____

5. *The History of Cartoons,* by Roger Funny was published by Color Press in Flower, New York in 1987.

   _____

6. *Rocks and Minerals,* by Roger Stone was published by Stone Press in Boulder, Colorado in 1989.

   _____

7. *Toys in History,* by C.R. Doll was published in Dollhouse, New York by Ragtime Press in 1989.

   _____

8. *Boats in History,* by Peter Sail was published in Wave, New York by Ocean Press in 1986.

   _____

WRITING A BIBLIOGRAPHY—THE BOOK

Read the information below. Then write it in the correct bibliography form.

1. *Baseball,* by Roger Base was written in 1989 and published by Diamond Press in Diamond, New York.

   _____

2. *Sports Legends,* by Richard Base was written in 1985 and published by Legend Press in Diamond, New York.

   _____

3. *Starfish,* by Linda Sea was published in 1989 by Wave Press in Oceanside, New Jersey.

   _____

4. *Plants and You,* by Lynn Budd was published in 1985 by Leaf Press in Stem, New York.

   _____

5. *Cars,* by Roger Wheel was published by Horn Press in Station, New York in 1993.

   _____

6. *Raising Your Puppy,* by C.W. Biscuit was published by Bow Wow Press in Spaniel, New York in 1989.

   _____

7. *Spacecraft,* by Peter Tripp was published by Ship Press in Travel, New York in 1986.

   _____

WRITING THE BIBLIOGRAPHY— THE MAGAZINE

Writing the bibliography for a magazine is much like writing one for an encyclopedia. First write the author's name (last name first). Then write the name of the magazine article in quotes. Write the name of the magazine and its date. Be certain to write its date. This helps readers to locate the magazine more quickly. Finally include the page numbers on which the article is found. Remember, put the magazine article name in quotes. Underline the magazine title and put the date in parenthesis.

Let's say that you found information about training parakeets in Pet Magazine in an article written by William Rogers in, "How to Train Your Parakeet" (April 7, 1989) on pages 85-87. How would you write it in proper form?

Write:

Rogers, William. "How to Train Your Parakeet." <u>Pet Magazine</u> (April 7, 1989), 85-87.

NAME _____

WRITING A BIBLIOGRAPHY—
THE MAGAZINE

Read the information below. Then write it in the correct bibliography form.

1. Your facts are from an article called "Snakes" by C. Slink in *Science Digest* (June 17, 1991) page 75.

    _____

2. Your facts are from an article called "Bicycle and Safety" by John Ride in *Hobby Digest* (June 13, 1993) on page 71.

    _____

3. Your facts are from an article called "Learning to Paint" by C.W. Brush in *Arts and Crafts* (June 21, 1992) on page 65.

    _____

4. Your facts are from "Rabbits and Gerbils" in *Pet Digest* (July 13, 1993) on page 63 by Roger Pet.

    _____

5. Your facts are from "Cars" in *Car Digest* (August 12, 1990) on page 48 by Peter Wheel.

    _____

6. Your facts are from "The Latest Fashion Trends" in *Teen Digest* (Sept. 1992) on page 99 by R. Dress.

    _____

7. Your facts are from "Eye Shadow and You" in *Teen Digest* (Sept. 1993) on page 33 by R. Lash.

    _____

WRITING A BIBLIOGRAPHY—
THE MAGAZINE

Read the information below. Then write it in the correct bibliography form.

1. Your facts are from an article called "Learning French" in *Language Digest* (Aug. 1991) by Peter Language on page 9.

    _____

2. Your facts are from an article called "Learning About Baseball" in *Sport Digest* (June 1990) by Roger Bat on page 10.

    _____

3. Your facts are from an article called "Cooking and Vitamins" in *Cooking Digest* (June 1993) by R. Baker on page 11.

    _____

4. Your facts are from an article called "Boats" in *Sport and Hobby Digest* (Sept. 1992) by R. Sail on page 12.

    _____

5. Your facts are from an article called "How to Raise Your Gerbil" in *Pet Digest* (Oct. 1991) by R. Cage on page 13.

    _____

6. Your facts are from "Fishing" in *Hobby Digest* (June 1993) on page 75 by R. Tackle.

    _____

7. Your facts are from "Planting Your Garden" in *Plant Magazine* (Oct. 1991) on page 65 by R. Spade.

    _____

WRITING THE BIBLIOGRAPHY— THE ENCYCLOPEDIA

The writing of the bibliography for an encyclopedia is slightly different from a book. Notice that the title of the encyclopedia article comes first in quotes. The title of the encyclopedia follows and then the year or edition. After the date comes the volume number and the pages the article is found on. This form gives the information quickly and easily at a glance. You know where the information was obtained. And notice that the year or edition is included. An article on snakes, may be in a 1985 edition but not in an 1986 edition of the same encyclopedia. So always include the year of publication when you write your encyclopedia bibliography. Remember to put the name of the article in quotations, and underline the title of the encyclopedia.

Let's say you find information about pirates in the *Encyclopedia of History* (1987) in an article called "Pirates."

How would you write this information in bibliographic form?

"Pirates." <u>Encyclopedia of History</u>. 1987. Volume 18, pp 188-91

WRITING A BIBLIOGRAPHY—
THE ENCYCLOPEDIA

Read the information below. Then write it in the correct bibliography form.

1. Your facts are from an article called "Washington" in the *Encyclopedia of American History* (1987) on page 11.

    _____

2. Your facts are from an article called "Starting Your Rock Collection" in *Encyclopedia of Science* (1989) on page 10.

    _____

3. Your facts are from an article called "The Jungle" in *Encyclopedia of Science* (1985) on page 31.

    _____

4. Your facts are from an article called "The Movies" in the *Encyclopedia of Arts* (1987) on page 39.

    _____

5. Your facts are from an article called "Space and Stars" in the *Encyclopedia of Science* (1987) on page 59.

    _____

6. Your facts are from "Training Your Parakeet" in the *Encyclopedia of Pets* (1986) edition on page 49.

    _____

7. Your facts are from "History of Cartoons" in the *Encyclopedia of Arts* (1989) edition on page 307.

    _____

NAME _____

WRITING A BIBLIOGRAPHY—
THE ENCYCLOPEDIA

Read the information below. Then write it in the correct bibliography form.

1. Your facts are from the *Encyclopedia of Science* (1989) on page 13 in an article called "Stars."

   _____

2. Your facts are from the *Encyclopedia of Science* 1992 on page 27 in an article called "Whales."

   _____

3. Your facts are from an article called "Sharks" in the *Encyclopedia of Science* (1989) on page 35.

   _____

4. Your facts are from an article called "Pirates" in the *Encyclopedia of History* (1987) on page 31.

   _____

5. Your facts are from an article called "Gerbils" in the *Encyclopedia of Science* (1986) on page 38.

   _____

6. Your facts are from the *Encyclopedia of Animals* (1986) in an article called "Making Friends With Animals" on page 211.

   _____

7. Your facts are from the *Encyclopedia of the Environment* in an article called "Learning About Your Environment" in the 1989 edition on page 65.

   _____

BIBLIOGRAPHY REVIEW CHART

It is important to use the same format throughout a bibliography.

BOOKS

Author
Title (underlined)
Place of publication
Publisher
Date

Example:
Johnson, James. Science for Kids. New York: City Press, 1993.

ENCYCLOPEDIAS

Author (if given)
Title of Article (in quotation marks)
Name of encyclopedia (underlined)
Edition
Volume
Pages

Example:
"Alaska," The World Book Encyclopedia. 1992, vol.1, pp. 102-109.

MAGAZINES

Author
Title of Article (in quotation marks)
Name of Magazine (underlined)
Volume:Number
Pages
Date

Example:
Smith, Joan. "Hunting Dogs," Field and Stream. 26:92-93, November, 1991.

PROOFING YOUR REPORT

Before you turn in your completed report, you need to go over your work to make sure no mistakes crept in as you were writing your final draft.

First, go in a private spot and read your report out loud to yourself. Quite likely, you will be surprised at how funny a sentence may sound when you hear it read.

Second, use this small "proofing checklist" to make sure that you have caught all the mechanical mistakes that you may have missed before. (These are mistakes having to do with punctuation, grammar, and spelling).

☐ Each sentence begins with a capital letter.

☐ Each sentence ends with a period, question mark, or exclamation point.

☐ Have checked the spelling of all words I am unsure of.

☐ Have checked for missing words in sentences.

☐ Name is on report.

Lastly, give your report to a parent or a friend to read. Ask them for feedback – is there anything that seems hard to understand, illogical, out of order? Sometimes when you've been working very hard on a written report it's hard to stand back and look at it critically. It's good to find someone who you can trust to read the paper and give you honest last-minute advice if needed.

MYSTERY

Missing people, dark shadows, mysterious strangers, footsteps in the night, strange occurrences – all of these mixed together make for a good mystery story.

In addition to these characteristics, there are several other factors that make a story, a mystery. The more of the following ingredients a mystery has, the better the story is likely to be.

Suspense – This is the nervous feeling you get while reading that something is going to happen, but you don't know what it is or when it will happen.

Clues – A good mystery should have clues so that you can follow the action and try to find out "whodunnit?"

Exciting plot – The storyline in a mystery should keep you flipping through the pages to find out what happens in the end. A good mystery should not put you to sleep!

False leads – A "lead" is information that can be of possible use to you in a search. False leads will keep you wondering by taking you off the path of where the real mystery lies. False leads will keep your suspense going as you read.

Mysteries are like puzzles. Using all of the "pieces" of what a good mystery should have, test the mysteries you read to see how they rate on the mystery scale.

READ A MYSTERY

Here is a list of mysteries that sixth grade children will enjoy.

Babbit, Natalie. *Kneeknock Rise.*

Bawden, Nina. *Devil by the Sea.*

Bawden, Nina. *Runaway Summer.*

Brandel, Marc. *The Mystery of the Two-Toed Pigeon.*

Brenner, Barbara. *Mystery of the Disappearing Dogs.*

Bulla, Clyde Robert. *Marco Moonlight.*

Bunting, Eve. *The Ghost Children.*

Carey, M.V. *The Three Investigators in the Mystery of the Trial of Terror.*

Christian, Mary Blout. *Sebastian (Super Sleuth) and the Purloined Sirloin.*

Clymer, Eleanor. *The Horse in the Attic.*

Craig, M.F. *The Mystery at Peacock Place.*

D'Ignazio, Fred. *Chip Mitchell: The Case of the Chocolate-Covered Bugs.*

Eisenberg, Lisa. *Mystery at Bluff Point Dunes.*

Farley, Carol. *The Case of the Vanishing Villain.*

Fleischman, Sid. *The Bloodhound Gang and the Case of the Secret Message.*

Giff, Patricia Reilly. *Have You Seen Hyacinth Macaw?*

Giff, Patricia Reilly. *Tootsie Tanner, Why Don't You Talk?*

Hahn, Mary D. *Following the Mystery Man.*

Hamilton, Virginia. *The Mystery of Drear House.*

Hildick, Clifford B. *The Case of the Condemned Cat.*

Hildick, Clifford B. *The Case of the Secret Scribbler.*

Hildick, Clifford B. *Manhattan is Missing.*

Hutchins, Pat. *The Curse of the Egyptian Mummy.*

Pantell, Dora. *Miss Pickerell and the War of the Computers.*

Roberts, Willo Davis. *Baby-Sitting is a Dangerous Job.*

Roberts, Willo Davis. *What Could Go Wrong?*

St. John, Wylly Folk. *Mystery of the Gingerbread House.*

Simon, Seymour. *Chip Rogers, Computer Whiz.*

Singer, Marilyn. *Where There's a Will, There's a Wag.*

Smith, Carol. *The Hit-and-Run Connection.*

Stevenson, Drew. *The Case of the Horrible Swamp Monster.*

NAME _____

MYSTERY RATING

Read a mystery story. As you read the story, think about the important parts of a mystery: suspense, clues, exciting plot, and false leads. When you have completed the book, fill in the information below.

Name of mystery: _____

Author: _____

(Rating System: 1=very poor, 10=excellent)

I would rate the suspense of the story: 1   2   3   4   5   6   7   8   9   10

I would rate the clues in the story: 1   2   3   4   5   6   7   8   9   10

I would rate the plot (storyline) of this story: 1   2   3   4   5   6   7   8   9   10

I would rate the false leads given in the story: 1   2   3   4   5   6   7   8   9   10

Look at the four ratings you gave your mystery. In which area was your story the strongest? The weakest? Write about the positive and negative aspects of the story below.

Positive: _____

_____

_____

_____

_____

Negative: _____

_____

_____

_____

_____

MYSTERY ACTIVITIES

1. **Write your own mystery.** Be sure to include believable characters, suspense, clues, and an exciting plot. Remember a mystery should be a story that people do not want to put down.

2. **Read and analyze a mystery.** Find a mystery book in your library. After reading the book write a short paragraph analyzing the following elements of a good mystery.
   - Did the story have believable characters?
   - Were the clues given helpful? Were there enough clues?
   - Was it an exciting plot? Was it hard to put the book down?
   - Were there any "false leads" given in the story?

3. **Illustrate your own mystery.** Choose a mystery and read it. When you have finished the book make an illustration on a poster, diagram, or any other form of art work.

4. **Present a mystery book to the class.** Pretend that you are a book salesperson. It is your job to sell the book to the kids in your classroom. Give a one minute talk explaining why the book is so good, but do not give away the ending. Convince the kids in your class that they should read this book.

CLASSIC CHILDREN'S LITERATURE

What is a classic? The dictionary says "an outstanding representation of its kind . . . having lasting significance or recognized worth . . a work generally considered to be of highest rank of excellence."

Many things are considered "classics" (or classical) in their categories. Classical music has been around for hundreds of years and yet is still purchased in music stores and listened to in concert halls and on the radio every day. Many old cars are considered classics because they have stood the test of time and are now extremely valuable. When you hear that clothing, shoes, furniture, and homes are "classic," this means that these things have remained in popularity over many, many years and now are still regarded as important and significant in today's society. The opposite of "classic" is "trendy" – something that is trendy is only popular, or in style for a short time.

Like all categories of things listed above, some books are also classics that have stood the test of time and are still being enjoyed today – even though several literary classics were written over a hundred years ago. Unlike many of the stories you read that are popular for a span of five or even ten years, a classic story goes through time remaining popular. Libraries and bookstores will keep ordering these books because they know they will never go "out of style." A new book may be very popular at the time of its publication, but as time goes by it will lose its popularity and will no longer be seen in libraries or bookstores.

Look at the list of books on the following page. Have you read any of these literary classics?

READ A CLASSIC

How many of these classic children's books have you read?

The Adventures of Huckleberry Finn by Mark Twain

The Adventures of Tom Sawyer by Mark Twain

The Adventures of Pinocchio by C. Collodi

Aesop's Fables

Alice's Adventures in Wonderland by Lewis Caroll

Andersen's Fairy Tales

Bambi by Felix Salten

The Birds' Christmas Carol by Kate Douglas Wiggin

Black Beauty by Anna Sewell

Charlotte's Web by E.B. White

Grimms' Fairy Tales

Heidi by Johanna Spyri

The Jungle Book by Rudyard Kipling

The Lion, the Witch and the Wardrobe by C.S. Lewis

Little Women by Louisa May Alcott

Mary Poppins by P.L. Travers

The Merry Adventures of Robin Hood by Howard Pyle

The Peterkin Papers by Lucretia Hale

Rebecca of Sunnybrook Farm by Kate Douglas Wiggin

Rip Van Winkle and the Legend of Sleepy Hollow by Washington Irving

Robinson Crusoe by Daniel DeFoe

The Secret Garden by Frances H. Burnett

The Story of King Arthur by Howard Pyle

The Swiss Family Robinson by Johann D. Wyss

Treasure Island by Robert Louis Stevenson

Twenty-Thousand Leagues Under the Sea by Jules Verne

The Voyages of Dr. Dolittle by Hugh Lofting

The Wind in the Willows by Kenneth Grahame

A True Classic

NAME _____

CLASSICS ACTIVITIES

1. Read one of the classics from the list. Write a paragraph stating why you think the story became a classic; what has made the story stand the test of time?

2. Many classic stories have been made into films. Read one of the classics that has a film adaptation. Compare the book with the movie. Which did you like better? Was the film honest to the book? What had been changed in the movie? Why do you think these changes were made?

   Classic book:_____ Author:_____

   What I liked about the book that I wish had been included in the movie:

   _____

   _____

   _____

   _____

   _____

   What I liked about the movie that I wish had been included in the book:

   _____

   _____

   _____

   _____

   _____

3. Pick one of the authors from the list of classics and write a short report about him or her. If you can, include details about what may have influenced the author to write the classic on the list. (Ask your librarian for resources that will give you information about the author of your choice.)

CHILDREN'S CLASSICS
HALL OF FAME

Nominate a story of your choice to the Children's Classic Hall of Fame. Write why you think the story you have chosen should become a classic.

_____

_____

_____

_____

_____

_____

_____

_____

_____

_____

_____

_____

_____

_____

_____

_____

_____

_____

_____

CLASSIC POETRY

Write a poem about one of your favorite classic children's story.

_____

_____

_____

_____

_____

_____

_____

_____

_____

_____

_____

_____

_____

_____

_____

_____

_____

_____

_____

_____

SUGGESTED AUTHORS FOR SIXTH GRADE

ADVENTURE
O'Dell, Scott

ANIMALS
Atwater, Daniel
Grahame, Kenneth
Lawhead, Stephen

FANTASY
Alexander, Lloyd

FICTION
Danizer, Paula
Zindel, Paul

HISTORICAL FICTION
Beatty, Patricia
Collier, James
Fitzhugh, Louise
O'Dell, Scott
Wisler, G.

MYSTERIES
Aiken, Joan
Moore, Ruth Nutton
Random House Alfred H. Hitchcock Series

SCHOOL STORIES
Asimov, Janet and Isaac
L'Engle, Madeline
Sleatur, William

THE GLOSSARY

1. *author card*—catalog card which is alphabetized by the author's last name.

2. *appendix*—any materials the author wishes to add to the body of the book such as tables or lists of information. It is found at the back of the book.

3. *bibliography*—an alphabetized list of books which gives the following information: author's name, source title, place, and date of publication, name of publisher and page numbers of magazine or encyclopedia article.

4. *body of book*—the main part of the book.

5. *book index*—an alphabetized list of topics/subjects that can be found in the book.

6. *divided catalog*—a card catalog divided into three sections: author, title, subject.

7. *card catalog*—a collection of cards arranged alphabetically by the author, title, or subject.

8. *character*—the animal, person, or nonhuman object in a story, play, poem or short story.

9. *climax*—highest point of tension in a story.

10. *copyright page*—found at the front of the book. It gives book title, author, publisher, place of publication, and copyright date.

11. *conclusion*—the end of the story, play, or short story.

12. *Dewey Decimal System*—system created by Melvil Dewey which arranges nonfiction books according to ten major divisions.

13. *dialogue*—conversations in a play, novel, or short story.

14. *encyclopedia cross reference*—found at the end of an article. It suggests other subjects to check under for additional information.

15. *encyclopedia guide words*—found at the top of the page. Topics are found alphabetically between these words used as guides.

16. *encyclopedia headings*—found within an encyclopedia article. Act like title headings for information in the article.

17. *encyclopedia index*—alphabetized list of subjects found in the encyclopedia.

18. *encyclopedia key words*—words under which you would most likely find information.

19. *encyclopedia see also references*—found at the end of an article. These subjects are additional subjects under which you can find information.

20. *entry*—information given under a word. Entries are in alphabetical order.

21. *footnote*—a note of reference or explanation which is placed at the bottom of a report page, giving the reader the information of where you specifically found your information.

22. *fable*—short, simple story which usually contains a moral or lesson.

23. *fairy tale*—simple story that has a hero, a problem and a happy ending.

24. *falling action*—story events leading to the ending.

25. *fantasy*—story that creates an imaginary world.

26. *fiction*—story which is not real.

27. *glossary*—a mini-dictionary of terms used in the book. It is found at the back of the book.

28. *guide letters*—letters placed on the outside of the catalog drawers that tell what cards are in the drawer.

29. *index*—an alphabetized list of topics/subjects that can be found in the book.

30. *media card*—catalog card used for vertical file, pamphlets, records, slides, or pictures.

31. *nonfiction*—story which is true.

32. *play*—story told by characters in dialogue.

33. *mystery* — a piece of fiction writing dealing with the solution of a mysterious crime.

35. *myth*—story which tells the trials and successes of a hero. It usually is a story created by people to explain something in life. Example: why it rains or snows.

36. *point of view*—the author's attitude toward the subject.

37. *preface*—a few words found at the beginning of a book (not all books have them) that explains ideas of the author such as why he wrote the book.

38. *research*—to investigate a topic thoroughly.

39. *science fiction*—fantasy story usually dealing with another time, another place, and often other beings. Definite rules do exist within the framework of this created world.

40. ***subject card***—catalog card which is alphabetized by the subject of the book.

41. ***table of contents***—listing of chapter titles found in the beginning of the book.

42. ***theme***—major idea of the story, short story, or play.

43. ***title card***—catalog card which is alphabetized by the title of the book.

44. ***tone***—the "feeling" of the written word, story, play, or poem.

45. ***vertical file***—a collection of small items too small to be placed on the library shelves. These may include pamphlets, newspaper clippings, pictures, posters.

NOTES

NOTES

NOTES

NOTES

NOTES